ATONEM

ATONEMENT
From Holocaust to
—— *Paradise* ——

Ulrich Simon

James Clarke & Co
—— Cambridge ——

CONIUGI DILECTISSIMAE HUIUS LABORIS OMNIS PARTICIPI

James Clarke & Co
P.O. Box 60
Cambridge CB1 2NT

British Library Cataloguing in Publication Data
Simon, Ulrich
   Atonement : from holocaust to paradise.
   1. Atonement
   I. Title
   232'.3   BT265.2

ISBN 0–227–67897–4

Made and printed in Great Britain by
The Guernsey Press Co. Ltd., Guernsey, Channel Islands.

Contents

INTRODUCTION

Twenty years have passed since I tried to come to grips with the unspeakable and the insoluble. For me, as a Christian theologian, Auschwitz had come to stand, as for so many, as a place on the map of Poland which would for ever symbolise all the woes and outrages of our time. There were other places of horror; indeed a litany can be compiled from Belsen through Maideneck to Treblinka and beyond. This despair arising out of catastrophe had moved me to find a note of hope somewhere. If atonement had ever meant anything at all it must be made to speak to our hearts. Redemption must be made effective. The twenty years which have passed have not lessened the task of my zeal and need to articulate reconciliation.

I did not die at Auschwitz, but I have shared the burden of the Holocaust. My father was murdered there in 1943. My brother had already been killed earlier in Stalin's terror. But these disasters are not confined to one's family. On the contrary, an uncountable throng of innocent victims pleads for remembrance. It is as if all the graves and pits of concentration camps and Gulags open and a universal cry is heard. The greater the indifference of the world the more intense becomes the cry. It is a cry not only demanding vengeance but also uttering a terrible threat. If the present chooses to ignore the past how will mankind fare? The trivial ordinariness of life stands in the dark shadow of violence and pain.

We have survived and enjoy the good life. How can one justify one's wellbeing? Food, clothes, shelter, friends, holidays, music and literature enrich our progress. But the virus has not left the body, for the continuance of terror since the second world war raises the doubt whether Hitler's atrocities can be confined to a unique period of criminality.

The complexity of the issue is immense. Terror and genocide are not academic questions. Indeed, we lack an agreed rational method for dealing with them. We can acknowledge and list the horrors and leave it at that. But we must also survey and take into account the happier issues which came after the defeat of the enemy. Reparations by the West German Republic, the emergence of the state of Israel, the entirely new climate surrounding Jews and Christians in their encounters, not to mention endless private experiences of reconciliation, yield an unprecedented credit. Theological reorientation has been drastic and the ecumenical bonds hold fast.

Yet Israel has also become the focus of irreconcilable tension and hatred. When I ended my book on Auschwitz the war of 1967 was not far off. Since then despite endless declarations reconciliation remains less attainable than ever. This may be felt not only between Jews and Arabs in Israel but throughout the world. The account remains unsettled, the bitterness remains. New demonic forces stimulate and profit from the armed contest. Auschwitz itself has become a place of pilgrimage inseparable from political propaganda. Yadwashem outside Jerusalem welcomes visitors to a shrine for the dead, but the detailed documentation in the museum gives no answer to the accursed Final Solution. The possibility of spiritual defeat stares us in the face even after the defeat of the enemy and the punishment of some of the criminals. Only the trees planted to commemorate the righteous among the Gentiles grant a shadow of consolation at Yadwashem.

The peril of spiritual defeat remains acute. Silence and ignorance must gladden the damned in their hell. But there is also the defeat of broken hearts. I have met many Jews, men and women, who having survived bear marks of indelible suffering. The remembrance of what happened has poisoned their souls. They cannot believe, they cannot hope, and they can hardly love. The bereaved, too, mourn without ceasing and without consolation. Even those less directly involved are tempted to capitulate to the very nihilism which Hitler and his gangs stood for.

Against this spiritual triumph of evil must be set the amazing growth of available knowledge. It has been a phenomenal intellectual event and shows no sign of ending. Research institutes have sprung up not only in Israel but also in Europe and in America, mostly attached to universities. Jews and Gentiles engage in studies of the Holocaust which are more detailed even than those carried out in compiling the *Encyclopaedia Judaica*. As in a court of law the interested parties can formulate the indictment on the basis of facts concerned with the crimes: committed at what time, in what manner, with what results and sometimes even by whom. To a lesser extent the same energy is displayed in nailing the crimes of the Stalinist murders and all the hideous outrages which have not lessened since the deaths of the two great tyrants.

Yet there is hardly a possibility of introducing a spiritual dimension to the past so precisely documented for our use. Indeed, there is even a resistance to any interpretation, for some researchers suspect an obfuscation of the facts. Another danger lurks behind this scepticism which favours an undeclared victory for the murderers. If a philosophical and a theological explication is not to be attempted the only conclusion to be drawn is that God does not exist. Goodness, truth and beauty are then tortured to death and the martyred dead witnessed in vain.

But how can God's ways to man be justified when we stand in the midst of violence? Where is evidence for goodness when rioters burn down houses, loot shops and kill peaceful citizens? Where is an intimation of truth when criminals control the media and terrorise the innocent? I stood at various points on the Berlin Wall and meditated in sight of the machine-gun posts and electric fences and patrol dogs on their leashes. Has not anarchy been institutionalised and is not oppression the index of our dehumanisation?

I shall avoid the cataloguing of outrages in the following pages. When they are mentioned the purpose is solely to stress the persistence of the guilt which has not been atoned, the presence of enemies not overcome, of revenge still looked for, of catastrophes not to be averted. I eschew with scorn the naïvety with which crime and punishment have been secularised and I oppose the pseudo-scientific theories which fail to honour the victims and appease the consciences of the survivors. Unless real atonement can be achieved the criminals succeed in murdering beyond Auschwitz and the Gulag Archipelago.

The ancient tradition of atonement has suffered in and through the holocausts. They have brought into disrepute the whole structure of religious sacrifice. The very name 'holocaust' – whole burnt offering – has a terrible and ironic ring. It promises nothing but disaster and destruction and is not linked to traditional values such as vicarious suffering, retribution, reparation, repentance, judgment and redemption. Instead sociological shibboleths have pushed out the inherited doctrines. Neither God and Christ nor the devil and his legions survive in the closed system of 'holocaust'.

This tradition, it must be said, had never been uniform. The first thing to be learnt about the doctrine of the Atonement in Christian theology is the fact that there never has been an agreed doctrine. Fortunately, the Councils of the Church never attempted to formulate such a test of orthodoxy. It was enough from the start, beginning with the New Testament, to assert that the work of Christ is central to the hope of reconciliation. This freedom in traditional theology is surprising. It encourages creative thought and also idle speculation. We are at liberty to look at the tormented face of Christ, the descent from the cross and the burial of the corpse, and see reflected in that victim the martyrs and victims of our world. But does such a reflection yield any result? And what could be the desired result?

In the first place it is admittedly therapeutic. We cannot abide the constant pain; we want wounds to be healed. Yet if we take the reflection beyond therapy far more is seen to be at stake. Just as the executed Jesus and the executioners opened vistas of eternal Atonement, so the bestial criminals and their innocent victims disclose not only the world in all its cruelty but our longing for the truth. The universal context matters as much as, if not more than, the passing event. I have been taught within the continuing stream of violence to stand aside from the endless pictures of horror.

Two influences may be noted by the reader, even if his or her experience may not be similar. These influences may at first seem to militate against the truth. First, there is the ever-growing ecumenical perspective which demands that whatever we may think from our own point of view is worthless unless it can be applicable within the world-wide community. Here we confront an obvious danger: ecumenical jargon leads to vagueness. Even if the global village does not exist, the truth must be global and more than global. Spatial limitations exclude atonement. The fences of Auschwitz and the walls of the Lubyanka cannot stand against the truth.

Secondly, the chronological and purely historical must be taken out of time. True, the prisoner groans in his cell in the long process of suffering. Hours go by as day follows day. Duration is torture in itself. Even sickness gives a taste of this imprisonment. Against this confinement in time, the possibility of atonement cuts across the unbroken cycle. Human beings, when *in extremis*, reach out towards the infinite. Only the eternal can satisfy our needs and remove us from the clocks ticking away in terror.

But this need forces upon us extra care, lest escapist fantasy replaces the hope of redemption. In order to transcend pluralistic vagueness of the liberal school and the monotony of Marxism, the vocabulary itself has to be refined. Sociology and psychology on the one hand, and Leninist agitprop on the other, have led into a kind of mental paralysis and will not lead out of it. But how can the rational truth be found if irrational forces confront us? The masters of truth did find such a way and encourage us on ours.

The immortals who dealt with reconciliation found forms in which to articulate atonement. It was rarely done in prose. Oedipus at Colonnae is reconciled and reconciles in dramatic poetry. Job seeks deliverance after breaking with God and receives the vision of God out of the storm. His soliloquies and the accusations use ancient forms. The dirge especially gives a sort of incantation to the theme of guilt and forgiveness. Elegies and funeral hymns are appropriate to our quest as well, if only to pair with the denunciations. Nor can we dispense with irony and all the tools of the literary craft. Since we are confronted with irrational forces we require the whole weaponry of language. Shakespeare and Goethe, for example, take us into the madness of demonic possession (in Lear and Faust) and transcend it.

But theologians resent this richness of approach. They even suspect reference to prose works, like Dostoevsky's or Solzhenitsyn's, as if novels provided an escape mechanism from serious issues. For example, Dillistone's splendid book, *The Christian Understanding of Atonement*, failed to make the mark it deserved because the author deployed the dimension of literature to help him in his task. But this blindness cannot continue in an age when even biblical scholars turn to 'narrative' as the key to understanding the gospels and Old Testament portions of scripture.

One play by Shakespeare seems to grasp the whole subject more cogently than any dogmatic treatise. It is *Measure for Measure*. It has been classed as a problem play, precisely because every character in this play, including the Duke, may be called flawed. Yet the criminal Angelo (the irony of the name!) is to be forgiven against his will after being discovered in his wickedness. How is guilt to be weighed? Measure for measure? If so, is it the quantity of sins or the quality of sin which must be computed? Shakespeare's incomparable genius never divorces this issue from the stage where things are happening, nor from the language through which they are happening. The play is the thing, involving us in, and yet also distancing us from, lust, corruption, lies, projected murder and betrayal and denouement of forgiveness and love.

My purpose cannot be to elucidate the wonderful complications of Shakespeare's play. But I continue to be concerned with *Measure for Measure*, with measures to comprehend guilt and the possibilities of reconciliation.

I

DEGREES

OF

GUILT

The world without guilt

A world without conflict, which we can no longer imagine, exists and flourishes around us. It is wholly without sin and guilt. It is more impressive than all the inhuman actions which we register. The despair of separation and the longing for reconciliation, in short the need for atonement, cannot be stated without our constant awareness of the visible, palpable and enjoyable order which rightly has been called wonderful and mysterious.

Open eyes perceive and keen ears listen to this order which is God's creation. The miracle of the natural order engages our senses. We look at the scenery around us: oceans, mountains, fields, streams, gardens and orchards, flowers and fruit in all their stages of growth. We enter their wonderful world and absorb their sounds and their silence. We touch them only rarely and do not really know them except indirectly. They reflect themselves in ourselves, as we study their organisation scientifically and love them aesthetically. Even untoward interruptions cannot destroy this natural order, for drought and flood, which annul fertility, storms and even decay pertain to this sinless universe. Nature is not a goddess but nature is of God.

Eyes and ears take us beyond this earth and above our solar system. The stars shine, whether we see them or not.

The light discloses an infinity of energy. The heavens declare the glory of God without containing or suggesting a fault. Just as the seasons on earth tell of everlasting change in changelessness, so the particles of stellar proportions correspond to the vast immensities in galaxies. This pre-established harmony comprises not one single order but a multiplicity of orders which cannot be destroyed or befouled. They reveal the cosmic context of our quest.

Even black holes and quasars, unknown to our fathers, do not flaw the goodness of the universe. Whether gardens of paradise or austere ranges of polar ice; planets, galaxies or cosmic wastes; small or immense spaces and energies; all these things interconnect. They depend on the creator and belong to the great chain of being. All depend on each other and structure the universe. They are not frozen, immobile or dead but change and continue to grow in the reflection of energy. The author of the book of Job would be amazed at how his vista of cosmic miracles would be enlarged by contemporary knowledge. But one thing has not changed; this is a universe free from guilt. Job is the forerunner of our quest in that he learns to hear and see that his leprous condition is put in perspective when the curtain rises upon the strange splendour around him. To forget this context is fatal in many respects, for then the political analysis of power blinds us. Without the stars in their courses and the invisible world of particles and radiation we are but cogs in a beastly machine, the worst of all possible worlds.

But the inanimate world of energy is not alone in its freedom from sin. Animals, reptiles, birds, fish and insects also belong to this hectic world of guiltless energy. They belong to the earthly evolution of life, multiplying and changing in the process of millions of years. But as we view this teeming richness we are alerted to distinctions. They may not be valid. Yet within the harmony of being, we welcome the vegetarians and do not know how to accommodate the meat-eaters which feed by killing. The list of creatures who fulfil their peaceful existence on earth, in the earth, above the earth, under the earth, in the sea, is almost endless. Their variety makes us marvel and we observe every species in detail. Their courtship, if any, mating and treatment of offspring dramatise for us a sinless existence, in no need of atonement.

This sinless wonder has been celebrated in poetry and music, such as Haydn's *Creation*. Both the wild and the domestic animals, the predatory and the song birds, the bees and the worms are 'very good'. The lowly and the great, from caterpillar to elephant, yield an enormous canvas of life which we do not only study but love. A world without a marmot on the rock, a hedgehog grunting along the ditch or a polar bear with her cub on her back would not be ours. We try to preserve threatened wildlife. No offence separates these creatures from us. Their innocence is at one with their exquisite beauty, their playful diversity confirms our view that within the chain of being a unity of purpose is reflected by all.

In this universe human beings have their place. More than that, they alone perceive the wonder of life in all its manifestations. Conceived by parents, born, playing, walking, seeing, hearing, speaking, maturing, loving, ageing and dying they also share in the process of reflecting the order. Mother and child portray the closeness and tenderness and the timeless quality of this mystery of life. The warm oneness can be translated into images. The mother holds, leans forward and feeds the child, and the baby clasps, drinks and smiles. There is no guilt in this dynamic harmony.

The child grows into manhood or womanhood. Here complete innocence is lost so that greater virtue may be gained. The young not only enter school and learn a trade or profession, but also confront choice and responsibility. How magnificent is the young man in quest of the world! How moving the young woman in her gentleness! Future fathers and mothers work towards courtship and parenthood. They learn to love, to lead and be led. Body and soul are touched by grace. An inner achievement complements the outward relationship. The embrace of the loving couple symbolises perfection, sparkling like a diamond, to be seen and to be admired.

This brave new world has intimations of eternity, for in the total surrender love reflects the light of the stars. Man and wife are without stain, erect, dignified, marvellous. Their continuance in bliss depends upon self-control or obedience to the eternal pattern of reality. They are fruitful in unbreakable bonds of fidelity. They are given power over the earthly creation as stewards. No atonement can be required when there is no separation. Beauty, goodness and truth radiate from this human existence based upon a constant love for the light which is supreme.

'What a piece of work is man! How noble in reason! How infinite in faculty! In form, in moving, how express and admirable!' Only when man's God-like glory is perceived in its infinite potential and as the miracle of evolution can the 'quintessence of dust' come as a shock. But even this dust does not spell out guilt and demand atonement if we view birth and death within the context of the pre-established harmony.

Conflict without guilt

The golden age no longer exists and we doubt even the strains of a pre-established harmony. Conflict, struggles, battles, killing and tormenting, destroy the peace and union of the world. Savagery intrudes incomprehensibly. If it is inherent in creation what does it reflect? We resent this dark side of creation. Its picture of the unbroken web of the cosmic unity dissolves and leaves no trace behind. We try to restore it without much success.

In our touchingly parochial way we try to account for the savagery by the food cycle. Life is lived at the expense of living things. Devouring flesh looks nasty and not fit for the Garden of Eden, yet who can find fault with the wild beasts who kill, and must kill, every day to stay alive? Do the lion and the eagle and the shark suddenly seem guilty of an offence? For us the sea in particular affords an alarming sight in which grotesque shapes move and catch their victims. There is a world of infinite complexity whose common purpose is capture and digestion. Reptiles bask motionless in the sun to lure their prey; sharp teeth dispose of that prey. Death is the destiny of life, for even the predators submit to violence. The strong beat the weak until they are overtaken themselves, sometimes by parasites or viruses, otherwise by old age.

How much these creatures suffer, or even resent their

fate, we cannot know. Domestic animals, however, evoke our sympathy. We see them rounded up and transported for slaughter. Pets enter even more warmly into our emotions though they are not sent to their death and are not part of the 'eat and be eaten' sequence.

Yet the human spirit registers and studies these rich varieties of conduct and destiny with happy equanimity. For some they do not disturb the created order. Haydn sets wild animals and vermin within the harmony of the created world, following the poets with their adulation of the greatest predators. Lions and eagles, tigers and falcons, whales and crocodiles, are acclaimed universally even if they are feared. Conflict there may be, but there can be no element of guilt when animals follow their instincts. Their conduct requires no atonement.

Some animals, however, make us pause and wonder, possibly because we shudder at their kind of killing. The piranha strips its prey, the snake paralyses its victim, the anaconda devours horribly, the weasel sucks the blood, the fox kills not to eat but for the sake of killing. Above all, and constantly before us, the ordinary cat not only stalks the mouse but plays with it, releasing it from its claws only to recapture it and then slowly terminate its life. There is terror here, and we cannot help wondering if nature, that unknown force, is tainted and perverted. The cat enjoys tormenting the mouse. If torture and torturing belong to instinctive behaviour, whence comes this instinct of cruelty? Where is responsibility to be placed?

We are not insulated against this enemy force, for our own bodies are also constantly under attack. The virus infection seems utterly purposeless; it breaks down our immunity and may kill for no reason at all. Far worse are the lives of those with bodies crippled from the beginning and minds vacant because of some imbalance in or after conception. But worst of all must be the slow dissolution of the body. Cancer is the lusty intrusion of cells which propagate themselves in an orgy of expansion and symbolically the disorder of cancer brings into question the order of the universe.

But such reactions on our part seem absurd. We come to

resemble the lady who stands before a Rembrandt and refuses to give her approval. The universe exists with its cruelties and cancers and invites no comment. It rejects comment by its silence. Our tears and plaints meet with no response. Even if with Job we rant against the order and long for death we are still defeated. But, strangely enough, death or non-existence is no alternative, for far from simplifying our quarrel the termination of life is for us a threat. We take avoiding action to retain life. Even Job does not seriously contemplate suicide. We, too, try to heal our diseases, combating cancer and organising rescue from accidents. We prolong this short life with heart transplants.

Nevertheless pain is not banished. There is throughout the living creation a giving and receiving of wounds, a taking and an offering of flesh, blood, and small organisms. It proceeds neither naturally nor peacefully. It looks to us like an ordeal. 'In the beginning was war' is a Greek saying of Heraclitus, and experience extends the axiom to almost everything. Yet although the whole creation accordingly groans, as St Paul acknowledged, no guilt can be identified. Even the cat and mouse game, repulsive as it is, lacks the elementary ingredient which causes guilt. The cat has no knowledge of its activity, no conscience by which to judge its conduct. Atonement does not seem to lie within the realm of the possible when instinctive behaviour not only causes division but authorises aggression and cruelty. Hence though we cannot identify guilt in this conflict we are not easy in our minds; there remains a lingering suspicion that something is wrong, out of order, perhaps natural and yet also unnatural.

The denial of human guilt

Although instinctive patterns of behaviour manifest a fight for existence, involving shocks, wounds, ordeals but no consciously vicious intention, human experience converges upon guilt. We know what we are doing, or at least we ought to know what we are doing. But at what stage of our life? And in what circumstances? The baby, the infant and the toddler are not deserving of blame; the young child and even the adolescent are not considered legally liable. The ageing, senile and confused may equally plead no or diminished responsibility. The disadvantaged and the disabled are not in the same category as normally equipped people. Hence relativism creeps into the moral fabric. The easiest way out of the problem of judging is to be wholly pragmatic and simply deal with 'cases' in the light of the circumstances. This reduces the concept of 'guilt' to an ambiguous quantity.

The facts, however, are not ambiguous. Human relationships are inextricably complex and never depart from the universal struggle. We not only share the animalistic urges and routines but refine and exaggerate them. For example, whereas some animals only propagate their species at limited times, the human species in its adult form remains sexually active throughout, thus propagating itself irrespective of food supplies. War is truly god of the race which makes devastations and calls them peace. The intention precedes the actual act, for a collective consciousness dominates the decision to make war. Conflict without guilt becomes guilt before and in conflict. Until recently the war had to be fought for survival, for as the human race evolved it had to subdue both hostile climate and savage animals. The seamless robe of creation had to be torn. Thus man became lord of the earthly dominion.

Only recently has the subjugation of animals been apprehended as a dubious victory. Cages and factory farming symbolise power over beasts bought at a price. On the one hand, the victory may turn out to be Pyrrhic in the sense that the food thus obtained is toxic; on the other, some humans are shocked by the methods employed. A few even realise that they touch here the surface of a much deeper guilt.

The denial of guilt nevertheless obscures other vast ranges of wrong. It will have none of the fall of Adam, as handed down in the Christian tradition. It refuses to acknowledge the sin of Cain, however many Abels are murdered in fratricide. The talk of envious siblings slides from cliché to cliché and hardly a day passes without reports of cruelty to children by their parents. Yet the sons of Cain turn a blind eye and a deaf ear to their own demonic and perverted nature. They are active, intelligent, inventive, devious, violent and insolent, but they are not guilty in their own eyes. The sons of Abel are without defence and are even accused of attracting violence, because they are withdrawn and passive.

The Christian tradition always insisted that the evil intention inspired sin. Guilt is not the outcome of a battle between equals, but the motivation for crime. Long lists of sins have been compiled in the past to give a systematic look to the chaos of evil. Pride and envy held the dominant position. These transcend animalistic acts of destruction. The envious individual, society, class or nation seeks to beat the envied and privileged. The envious not only identifies but also hates the other. This is the sin of Cain. Reconciliation is the last thing he seeks. He develops a lust which will not be satisfied except through the death of the victim.

The drama of human history is the action inspired by envy and hatred. Cain victorious yields only to Cain more powerful, younger, stronger and cleverer. After his triumph the conqueror remains aggressor, killing in order to secure his position. Traitors and spies must be recruited and rewarded. But even security is empty unless the triumphant Cain is applauded, flattered and worshipped. The Beast on the throne demands total surrender and rules by fear and favour until he too is overthrown or dies. This Satanic figure never acknowledges trespass, sin or guilt.

The biblical and Christian tradition has never been at a loss to set historical faces to the Satanic usurper of the creator. Cain, Belshazzar, Judas, Nero and Muhammed are the dark patrons of the Inferno with whom Abel, Daniel, Jesus, Peter, Paul and all the saints have no traffic. The former enjoy inflicting tortures; the latter endure them. The former murder in orgies of lust and self-exaltation; the latter suffer and win crowns of glory. In our own day a Hitler struts across the stage of triumphs, a Bonhoeffer is hung on the gallows; the former commits suicide and is burnt in flames of petrol, the latter looks radiantly at his enemies. No compromise is sought or given.

According to the Christian faith, this brutish parody of power cannot be eligible for reconciliation, for it is a sham, a nothing, despite its temporary terror. It is condemned and subject to retribution. The reversal of power exposes the guilt of the wicked. Thus Babylon, the harlot of nations, must capitulate to the true Jerusalem.

But in the monolithic structure of the socialist state, hatred and violence are accepted as part of the class warfare. The propagandists elevate struggle to be the norm, part of a scientific theory. Alleged anti-social behaviour is a crime to be punished. The charges have nothing to do with sin, trespass and guilt, for socialist theories scorn a spiritual or ethical content. This denial acquits the butchers of all atrocities.

This acquittal is a form of the *realpolitik* which is not confined to Nazi outrages or to Marxist-Leninist legality. Liberalism had developed the inherent trend with its at first tentative, and soon blatant, reform programmes. 'All things are permitted' allows mankind to legislate for itself. To this end the stakes become ever greater. For example, the liberation of sexually repressed women ends in charters of freedom, which permit female children to apply for birth-control pills, to demand abortion when pregnant and thus to engage in total promiscuity. Anything can be sanctioned for 'the good cause', which means employment, profits and even the destruction of the environment. Violence, too, receives its sanction from the liberal premise that the right to demonstrate involves the freedom to break down, to trample upon, to burn, to steal, to set up anti-authority by any means. The brutalisation of towns by noise and pollution is accepted as normal. The evil intentions, which turn laughing children into raping, killing and lying adults, are no longer indicted as spiritual deformities, for the depravity of the soul is excluded in liberal philosophy as in Marxist sociology.

Atonement does not arise in behaviourist circles. Comparing humans with caged animals or conditioned species, it measures the latent energies and reflexes in experiments. The denizen of the rat world ousts, abuses, bites and conquers other rats in order to gain first place. Terms such as 'repentance' and 'forgiveness' are out of place. Even the element of pleasure, the sadistic streak observable not in rats but in men, can be 'explained', for it is normal behaviour. A Mengele who acts as angel of death at Auschwitz not only consigns men, women and children to gassing and to torture, but also enjoys his job. A woman communist in the camp enjoys screwing the last ounce of energy from her starving workers in the clay pits. Rats only bite, humans torment. Behaviourism registers this behaviour without censure.

Guilt cannot be established when the torturers are the judges and the victims the accused. As in Collodi's *Pinocchio*, when the puppet is arraigned for having been robbed, a parody of justice threatens our existence. This perversity seems to us new and perhaps unprecedented, although history does not lack instances of gross terror. *Macbeth* is rightly cited as exemplifying the suppression of fair by foul in the murdering by the host of his guest. But Macbeth and, even, Lady Macbeth suffer from the effects of their deeds. They do not acknowledge their guilt or seek reconciliation, but they know themselves to be guilty. As the play proceeds and they lose their hold on themselves they lose the power to control events. Their guilt need not be demonstrated: it is there for all to see.

The Macbeth corporate state, however, is not so easily terminated, for its terror continues even beyond the lifetime of the murderers. The list of GPU-KGB chiefs reads like a dynasty of Neros. Some of them (Yeshov and Beria) were themselves murdered, but their machines suffered no harm. Only once, under Krushchev, was an admission of guilt for past outrages actually heard from a Soviet Politbureau forum. The thaw did not last long. Few Nazi war criminals and no Japanese general ever expressed more than vague regret for the past.

Christians intervene in this sombre pageant by offering penitence. For example, immediately after 1945 the Protestant churches in Germany passed a resolution of confessing their guilt. They had not murdered or condoned murder, but they had failed to stop the murdering. Similarly other western religious bodies acknowledged their share in moral disasters. Sometimes these resolutions seem vague and cheap when measured against the total. When millions have lost all, the residue of guilt can no longer be quantified. We do not even know whether the present age outstrips the past in percentage terms in the administration of injustice and torture. But we are not really concerned with numbers or percentages when we focus upon guilt. The denial of guilt is certainly the most horrifying aspect of Cain's heritage: 'Am I my brother's keeper?'

Healing human guilt

Not all psychologists side with behaviourism. Indeed, most clients consult psychologists because they connect their troubles with some unknown but real enemy within. Psychologists, therefore, face guilt as a disease from which they may offer release. Some psychologists even permit a religious dimension to their therapy, but this is unusual, if only because the beginnings of psychoanalysis were grounded in atheism. Freud's task, as he saw it, was to liberate not only his clients but the enlightened world from the illusion of religion. He drew upon some ancient strands of human culture in the west or rather the Mediterranean, and universalised specific complexes of guilt. Curiously enough for a Jew, he did not popularise the one story and tradition in the scriptures which would have served his purpose of secularising the sacred. The Cain and Abel narrative leads up to the *Aqedah*, the horrific binding of Isaac by his father Abraham, and a vast amount of commentary has been written and handed down during the post-biblical centuries. No story in the Bible dramatises as briefly the chasm that opens up between father and son. Yet Freud's fame does not rest upon his interpretation of this material, nor has his treatment of Moses been received with acclamation. As against this, Freud's approach to violence, guilt and suffering is celebrated for his theoretical and clinical application of the myth of Oedipus. Perhaps it was easy for a Jew in the Vienna before Hitler to mirror the soul's sickness in the work of Sophocles. More important than this choice is the principle behind it. Once the doors to the past open, not only Oedipus but also Agamemnon, Antigone and Philoctetes give a framework to the portrayal of guilt and to our search for reconciliation. Similarly the pages of the Old Testament may be opened and reveal the need for atonement. What could be more telling than the story of Joseph and his brothers?

The object of treatment is healing. This is no longer obtained in the conventional manner of a confession of sins and a promise to do penance and give up the wrong way of life. Nor is absolution looked for. Yet the secular process is not altogether divorced from this pattern. The psychiatrist or analyst is central to the proceedings. He listens to words which may be uttered spontaneously or may be an attempt to give a report of dreams. As he listens the words convey to him the burden of the guilt. He offers himself to act as a priest and even as a victim in sharing the guilt. Transference is certainly a priestly vocation and a costly undertaking. It does not become less costly because the therapist ultimately restores, and desires to restore, the independence of the client.

The therapeutic venture is also costly for the patient. In the first place, he must pay for the treatment. Like the petitioner in the days of the Temple he must have something in his hands to give. But more painful is the realisation that the treatment uncovers depths of unconscious wounds, griefs and all sorts of evils; no single surgical operation can remove the offending article. One may laugh at the expression 'opening a can of worms', but it is true that unlike the penitent who has prepared his confession and no more, the patient in analysis has to go much further in stripping himself down. There are no defences.

If the treatment is to succeed, it demands from the patient an intellectual awareness as part of the response. After all, if he enters into the ancient mythology he must also understand what it means to want to slay a father, like Oedipus. More than that, he must identify with Oedipus so as to arrive at his peace at Colonnae. All tragedies begin with the fall of flawed characters; hence all treatment must reveal the hidden guilt.

In such treatment the accent varies greatly, but the guilt in question is only rarely seen as the result of sin. The moral question may never be put. Even homicide may receive its explanation in terms of prenatal conditioning, postnatal circumstances and even chemical imbalance. Every case differs, and every therapist brings a different cultural background to the work of reconciling the patient to himself. The matter becomes even more complicated when in family contentions, such as divorce, more than one patient is involved and reconciliation cannot be achieved.

Freud's obsession with sex and sexual disturbances seems to have removed the psychological understanding of guilt from the traditional orbit of atonement. Adler's orientation towards power and inferiority widened the perspective. Jung went much further and without reverting to a Christian or Jewish biblicism set the struggle of the soul in a less individualistic limitation. A patient in Jungian analysis becomes aware of the collective unconscious. In a sense his guilt is lessened, for he stands between opposing forces and, like Adam and Eve in the Genesis story, is destined to a struggle in a dualistic universe. The task and purpose of life is to achieve individualisation and to rise to maturity. A Jungian psychology does not deny the impact of demonic assaults and demands a spiritual knowledge beyond the appearances of the ephemeral world. As regards atonement and forgiveness, little remains in this somewhat Faustian world. Just as Goethe's Faust emerges from murder, seduction and fraud, to be received into bliss in view of his endless striving, so Jung answers Job not by justifying God's ways to man, but by accusing God on behalf of man. Once Job is drawn into psychological patterns a new perspective seems to open to the healing of human guilt. Could it be that God, or the universe, has a share in guilt? If so, what becomes of the Christian claims of Atonement?

As long as healing stands as the imperative necessity, such theological questions cannot arouse much interest. The main thing is for the self to get rid of its bondage, for the shadow of the self, to speak in Jungian terms, to be integrated. I have often listened to educated men and women telling how they came to 'accept' themselves and thus their real or alleged guilt. The somewhat fantastic theosophy of Jung, of a quaternity instead of the Trinity, never registered with patients or indeed with philosophers. But the problem of evil, as we shall see, will not go away when one clinical case has ceased to be painful.

The success of this therapy is strictly limited to people of good will. The patients are generally not criminal and do not belong to the cadres of the secret police and torturers. They are sensitive souls who want to 'work through' their guilt, for their consciences are tender. As Jung so rightly maintains, they are and have souls, even if their souls are sick. Those who administer the therapy are equally intent on achieving a wholeness for split personalities and on removing obstacles that militate against wholeness.

Where no such good will obtains psychological therapy does not exist. There individuals lose their names and their identities, and without being criminals they are degraded as if they were. In most countries with a tyrannous regime hospitals and prisons administer a policy which violates the dignity of persons. Individual guilt cannot survive when law and psychiatry pervert not only justice but also normal existence. Jung was intuitively certain that this collective phenomenon issues in a machinery of terror. This new impersonal determinism has its own momentum. It also challenges us to resume the quest for healing and wholeness.

Variables of guilt

Atonement with the goal of reconciliation is now unworkable unless the complexity of guilt is taken into account. Clearly a person-to-person strife involves wholly disparate levels of antagonism. For example, a cool business-like competition, which aims at damaging another, is not in the same class as a carefully planned murder. An uncharitable nastiness, which engages in slander and insults, cannot be compared with a sadistic rape or kidnap. The cases taken to court, which present only a small sample of ills, are never wholly alike and though they are judged by precedents they demand detailed evidence to underline differences.

In person-to-person quarrels and plaints motivation is of more interest to the theologian than the immediate and factual evidence of deeds done. Yet the why, i.e. the cause behind the crime or injury, is almost as complex as the deed, if not more so. Motivation cannot be established easily, for even a confession, if it can be obtained, may be as misleading as an interview. We may ask 'Why did you burn your neighbour's house?', or 'Why did you rape this young woman?' and either receive no answer or a reply which is evasive and intended to cover up an evil and disgusting madness. I remember the theological student who on being arrested after exploding a small bomb in Westminster Abbey said: 'One's got to do something'.

Despite the complexity of individual motivations and the unreliability of statements they enable us to make sense of atonement. As long as there remains an I-thou relationship not only can we identify in some measure with both, but we can also detect levels of interacting desires. These pertain to the core of human existence. Classical systems have shown them to be capable of both good and evil. This systematisation has obtained for centuries and may now look a little artificial. Nevertheless the structure of the seven sins attracts us still by providing a solid base to the chaotic confusion of contemporary alienations. Moreover, this structure scores by offering also a positive view of human desires, pairing the sinful abuses with gifts and virtuous achievements.

Thus free choice and, therefore, responsibility, govern human beings as they decide for themselves between virtue and sin. Pride seeks and fulfils itself in humility, envy in charity, anger in temperance, laziness in fortitude, avarice in generosity, gluttony in sobriety, lust of all kinds in purity. The numbering of the spirals or circles of sins (as in Dante's *Divine Comedy*) need not detain us, nor should the labelling of the corresponding virtues be taken too literally. Their value lies in stressing the openness of our existence, the motivation behind our deeds and the freedom which governs our destiny. Through the provision of this balanced reality of layers upon layers of desires guilt ceases to be a fixed thing, to be quantified only in terms of offence. Rather guilt now pairs with lost virtue, alienation with lost membership, anarchy with order. Accordingly atonement, instead of being seen as a single act of legal reconciliation, answers to the complex variables of guilt.

Guilt in Aristotelian and in Scholastic terms lies in all manner of excess. If we follow such schemes we have to become reconciled not only to active offences but also to passive omissions. Virtue lies in the middle. But the traditional listing of virtues goes beyond that, in as much as after the cardinal or natural virtues (fortitude, justice, temperance, prudence), faith, hope and charity light up a transcendental glory to which no vices can correspond.

There is, therefore, a limitation to the variables of guilt. But two negative factors drag us down and lessen our confidence in atonement. Above all, there is an abstract quality about both vices and virtues which fails to correspond to the matter in hand. We still want to probe into the recesses of motivation. Why do pride and envy feed the proud and envious? How do the angry and lazy acquire their liking for their sin? What causes human beings to lust after goods, alcohol, drugs and human flesh? As soon as we question in this manner we are back with the criminals. Face-to-face with another abstract, guilt ceases to be a meaningful concept.

More to the point, however, remains the irrelevance of this whole approach to the kind of impersonal and conditioning evil which taints all moral distinctions. Lacking a face it cannot be met face-to-face. The Marxist-Leninist *apparatchik* typifies the facelessness which rejects even the abstract notions of goodness. But the facelessness of institutions is not restricted to one political spectrum. The universal nothingness and its nihilistic contempt of virtue cannot even aspire to have the characteristics of the seven or any other sins. Whereas even pride, envy and all the rest conjure up some sort of personality, the KGB, Gestapo, security forces everywhere and camps Gulag and otherwise, only symbolise lies, fraud and cruelty. The only dimension appropriate to this hell is nothingness. Meaningless horror has no variables of guilt. It breaks the cosmic balance and order.

II

VISIONS

OF

HELL

The pact with the devil

In view of the heavy odds against a happy life and a restoration of harmony, it cannot surprise that men and women capitulate to evil and enter hell defiantly. The war criminals of our time and the liquidators of millions are perhaps not as original as we like to think. There is a long line of sinners who actively promote the affairs of the City of Destruction. But even within their ranks there remains a huge variableness. Thus we know little of the lesser and mean spirits who oppress and torture and defraud others. The famous names have become known as symbols of diabolical stature and they appear in a hierarchic devilry. According to Dante's structure of the Inferno, these boastful impenitents continue as shades in their former identity and engage more voraciously than ever in futile nothingness. Thus they are damned and opt for damnation. Dante peoples the circles of damnation with heroes, kings, princes, philosophers, lovers; with gluttons, hoarders, spendthrifts; with murderers of all kinds. But even more close to the principle of evil are the perverters of the truth, the heretics who know themselves that they are frauds. These criminals against nature and art are not less violent than the murderers, but far more successful in violating the heart of reality. Suicides, blasphemers, sodomites, seducers, sorcerers and falsifiers occupy the lowest hell; it

THE PACT WITH THE DEVIL

does not lack distinguished residents. such as popes and emperors. The traitors complete the picture: Judas, Brutus and Cassius conspire to end the universe as created by God.

In this Hell there can be no reconciliation but only punishment. The punitive measures are mostly borrowed from Greek mythology. Minos, Cerberus, the Furies, Gorgon and Geryon whip and chase their victims over burning sand and pitch them into a boiling bubble of viscous glue. Illustrators have seized upon the text and translated it into almost unbearable pictures. Botticelli takes the viewer along with Virgil and Dante to descend into scenes of horror where the naked villains pursue their course, plunging into holes in vain attempts to escape from black bitches. The pack springs on the violent with open fangs. But though they are torn limb from limb their pain and sorrow never end. The violent has made for himself a gibbet from his own lintel.

There is no end to these futile spasms in rivers of excrement. After the heat comes the extreme cold. Behind Dante lies the dark wood where he was lost and where leopard, lion and she-wolf stood in his way. Now he knows that all is lost for ever among the impenitent. But we are taught even more than the dramatic pictures show, though they hint at the inner and spiritual betrayal of God, self and society. Satan eats his servants with rake-like teeth, but Satan's eternal dinner consists of the food which the traitors will to offer. The pact with Satan is consummated in total chaos and night. The only existing tie is that of sly and cruel hatred. In that sense the Satanic allegiance achieves its goal in that the haters are turned, or turn themselves, into permanent hatred. They are their own executioners for their free decision is now fixed.

But as for Hell, questions had to be raised: Why must this be so? Are not the stench and the din a projection of idle fears? Or do the fumes and the roar simply act as inventions to uphold doubtful morals?

Dante's Inferno did not condemn penitent evil-doers, for they passed into Purgatory where they willed to redeem their debts by suffering and receiving forgiveness.

Purgatory was then a school of charity, the beginning of a forward movement towards bliss. The horror of Hell lay behind the pilgrims who, like Dante himself, had forsworn Satanic allegiance.

But this optimistic scheme of salvation did not prevent pessimism from gaining the upper hand. Fear certainly acted as a common link when the Black Death and other scourges devastated Europe. Could anyone escape from the ultimate punishment? The *Dies Irae* of Thomas of Celano even preceded these catastrophic events and Dante's optimistic vision. Its hold on the people lasted for centuries, if only for its haunting theme of wrath and doom. The sound of the trumpet rings through the sepulchres and universal death follows. The book has a record which acts as evidence before the righteous judge. Evil men and evil deeds will be avenged. Even the just stand in need of mercy. Only the judge himself, Jesus, God incarnate and sacrificed, can on appeal rescue the lost from unending woe. Sin's pollution can be wiped away by absolution. The suppliant is guilty but pardoned, yet the prospect is bleak unless the atonement is attained by tears and submission.

The threats in the Church's sacramental and pastoral office lost their force. Public feeling reacted against both the pressures and the promises of Atonement. Hell and heaven receded gradually after the Reformation. The Enlightenment went about salvation in a different way and the pact with the devil could be reinterpreted. But this took time as the centuries passed and societies changed.

Christopher Marlowe, born in 1564, was still in his twenties when he wrote his *The Tragical History of Doctor Faustus*. He did not invent the plot of the pact with the devil nor the interest in magic. The original Faustus was probably a quack of some sort who sold horoscopes and quite possibly violated boys. At any rate, that Faustus had become a stereotype of devilry and an object of hatred. But curiously the shadowy figure became fused with the spirit of the age as represented by Paracelsus, who saw in the 'light of nature' a second revelation, next to the 'light of grace'. Orthodox dogmatists refuted as devilish his teaching, which speculated on nature as a divine channel of secret knowledge, and thus the connection with Faustus was made. This new striving after the wisdom of the All, the *Pansophia*, interested itself in chemistry as part of a titanic longing after a scientific entry into the cosmos. But the popular Faustbook in Germany is merely anecdotal, farcical and legendary, drawing even upon such ancient themes as Helen of Troy. The stuff belongs to the puppet theatre of the times where a bit of moralising helps things along.

When Marlowe got hold of this strange mixture, he strengthened the titanic strain and retained the farcical interludes. His Faustus signs the pact with the devil and obtains supernatural powers; he masters the spirits, exercises his power in politics and receives the finest of all women. He knows no limits in seizing life at its fullest and scorns the consequences. The present, not the future, matters to him, for he acts as a god on earth. Yet Scenes XIV and XVI prepare for the final defeat of the titan. The 'face that launch'd a thousand ships' cannot save him when the reckoning comes, and there is a reckoning. Time conquers and midnight approaches, too late for repentance: 'See, where Christ's blood streams in the firmament! One drop of blood will save me: O my Christ.' It does not save, the soul is lost, damnation is eternal. Repentance made of fear alone does not avail.

This treatment of Faustus is only the prelude to a momentous polarisation: on the one hand, fear of death (*timor mortis*) and loss of soul prevail, as, for example, in the English Book of Common Prayer with its pessimistic view of sin and the uniquely compassionate work of Christ; on the other, there is this lively interest in the natural world and soon the rise of natural science. We cannot tell how people felt except in the reflected light of literature, art and music. Even among the parties, such as the Puritans and Pietists in Europe and later in America, extremes of hope and despair may be found. The genuine Christian voice sings its tune most convincingly in hymns, chorales and, above all, in Bach's cantatas early in the eighteenth century. It rises above and beyond extremes.

However, Faustus never ceased to haunt the European mind. Though damned and damnable, he is the passionate seeker who gains in status, as cosmic theories of Bruno and Kepler and the philosophies of Descartes, Spinoza and Leibniz percolate through the universities. Marlowe's Faust belonged to the repertoire of the travelling theatres. The young growing Goethe saw Faustus on the stage in Frankfurt and fascination for him never left the genius throughout a long life. By 1790 he had already completed the first draft of *Faust part I* and thus aroused a new interest among friends. Again two disparate themes unite on a higher plane: the determination to reach, possess and teach pure truth, despite the possibility of error; and the will to exercise unprecedented power, albeit by doubtful, diabolic means. Others, mostly forgotten, elaborated the Faustus mixture and ended with the hero's descent to hell, always a telling finale on the stage. Not so Goethe, who right from the start links his Faustus with Job. The Almighty God tries his servant, and the Satan, now Mephistopheles, strikes a bargain, gambling upon the heedless adventurer's recklessness. In Goethe's *Faust* the soul of humanity is at stake. Can Faust be Faust and still be a child of God, in harmony with the cosmic order?

Goethe's Faust from his first appearance is the questing seeker. All he knows of the gamble is stipulated in his pact with the devil. His soul will be forfeited immediately if at any time he is so content as to say to the moment, 'Abide, please, you are so lovely'. And there are many moments which could elicit such a response. The triumphs of magic soon recede; the seduction of the innocent girl is almost forgotten; immense experiences which are beyond time and space, first in the German mountains, then in Greece; political and military exploits leading up to the utopian settlement of a free people on free soil – all these transcend the existing Faust phantasmagoria. Even the marriage with Helen after the descent into the underworld and the birth of their child who dies in soaring flight cannot undo Faust's restless striving. To the grumbling and cynical annoyance of the devil, Faust's demands still increase. So much has happened and so much is also forgotten that the spectator or reader may be inclined to dismiss the pact with the devil and to lose sight of damnation or salvation. What had begun theologically has ceased to be the justification of man before God.

The final and fifth act of *Faust part II* finally lays to rest traditional interpretations of atonement and opens the way to salvation in a manner which was to become normative for a century in Europe. Goethe had already composed the outlines of the climax by around 1800, but he only completed the grand design shortly before his death, i.e. in 1831–2. He had already conceived the decisive step of converting the damnation of Faust into the salvation of this protagonist of the new world of power and technology. It seems almost unbelievable that the scene could have been set before the invention of steam and electric power, let alone nuclear. For power is the key to the drama.

Power conditions freedom and is utterly ruthless. Philemon and Baucis own a hut and in their modest happiness and contentment represent the old religion. In simple verses and with childlike rhymes they unfold the serenity of a fulfilled old age, safely hidden in limitation. Theirs is the idyll which is threatened by Faustus and his grand design. Their little possession is in the way and so are the trees and the chapel and the contemplative life. Ahab's sin, the murder of Naboth and the expropriation of the vineyard (1 Kgs. 21), is being repeated with brutal means and monotonous triviality: the three hooligans do their job and will continue to terrorise in the Mephistotelian scheme of Faustian expansion. Faust rejects the intimations of conscience and though blinded by care he will not be influenced by this lulling voice. But guilt does remain. Faust is himself cheated by the cheating devil, for being blind he interprets the noise of the 'bulldozers', shovelling in the marshy earth, as part of his scheme. But this reclamation is not for new settlements: his grave is being prepared. The tragic irony is complete. The dream of fertile soil for new communities becomes the reality of death. Faust, the magician's debtor, never cared at all for peaceful community nor had he ever worked with his hands. Moreover, Faust, like Goethe, never believed in 'the people'. His anticipation of success is illusory, if only because Mephistopheles already schemes to return the dehydrated dunes to the sea. The nihilist, who achieves the total void after the failure of ceaseless activity, mockingly wins.

And yet Mephistopheles finally loses. Though Faust finishes life aged a hundred years with a debit balance of guilt and still enticed by illusions of success, the devil cannot capture his soul. Goethe's tragedy ends in death, but not in damnation. Mephistopheles has kept his side of the bargain and has every right to draw what remains of his partner into the eternal void. Nothing should come between the powers of hell and the Promethean activist, the magician of modern times. He has forfeited the right to appeal for he has never cared about his soul's salvation. He has daily conquered the inner and outer limitations to life. At the end in his blindness he has enjoyed the highest moment of existence and confessed his willingness to say to that moment: 'Stay, abide!' This willingness is somewhat qualified: Faust *could* say 'abide', and thus lose the gamble according to the pact signed in blood.

But this legalistic aspect of the case need not be taken too seriously. Goethe enjoys the humorous side of 'cheating the devil', just as previous writers had done. We also still smile approval at the devil's failure to cash his bond in view of the linguistic escape clause. Faust did not say 'abide', but he could have said it, thus sealing his doom.

Forgiveness and atonement, however, move on a more demanding level of moral responsibility. Though Mephistopheles may lose his prey because he is too stupid and lacks the skill of catching a soul and the power of using the powers of hell, so that his perverse lust fails, how can we condone the acquittal and redemption of the unrepentant seducer and murderer Faust, the prototype of the modern age? As Mephistopheles curses the intervention from above, the waving and weaving of choirs of angels in clouds of rose petals which force his retreat, he challenges us with his appeal to justice. Every effort in this absurd business has been frustrated by love.

And loving intervention it is! But is it morally justified? It is impossible to reproduce here the lyricism of that last scene: mystics, saints, children, angels, the beatified penitent women of the New Testament precede the *Una Poenitentium*, the Gretchen of *Faust part I*, who after having been seduced had killed her mother and child unwittingly, and had then been arrested, tried, and executed. She intercedes on behalf of her former lover, who had forgotten her existence. It is a Catholic ending in which adoration and thanksgiving blend in perfect harmony. The temporal parable is consummated in eternity: salvation and not damnation is the end of the great sinner, who can be and is redeemed because always he laboured with unceasing striving. For this he can be 'met from above', grace crowning nature.

How is it possible to deny Goethe the entirely Christian character of such an ending? True, he himself never claimed allegiance to an established church or dogmatic formulation. But what is Christian if not this amazing encounter of the rising spiritual world with the eternal love which gives unconditional grace? Even tender repentance, itself a gift from God, opens the eyes to the vision of unspeakable bliss. No dogmatic theologian could evoke more movingly the irresistible work of grace which purifies, transforms, and welcomes the soul. The frescoes of the Campo Santo in Pisa and the iconography for Dante's *Divine Comedy* furnish the sharply edged figures of the hierarchical and sacred Godhead with Christ, Mary and the saints.

In this ascent the redeemed Faust ceases to be the individual with a criminal past and rises to represent the humanity which reflects God in his creation. Much falls away into oblivion and insignificance, but the kernel of genuine effort remains.

The theodicy seems complete: God justified to man and man justified by God. Yet doubts have always been voiced, not only by Protestant and Catholic dogmatists. It is, strangely enough, on moral grounds that the sensitive conscience finds itself repelled by the salvation of Faust. After all, the diabolical outrages were directed against and not for humanity. His was by no means the undiluted good will which obeys the categorical imperative. On the contrary, he defied the Kantian Practical Reason, the ethical framework which alone produces peace and concord among men. If Faust is universal man and is ultimately blessed with restoration and rewarded with eternal love, the way is open to indifferentism all round. Theologically speaking, the cross of Christ is not needed and reconciliation is obtained without sacrifice.

It is precisely this secularisation of redemption which endeared Goethe's Faust to the liberal sentiment of European enlightenment. Here at last was salvation not within but outside the Church. In many homes the ending of Faust was read aloud at Christmas or on New Year's Eve. The feeling at such a reading was devotional, as if the audience identified with Faust. After all, these men and women throughout the century after Goethe, i.e. until 1933, were striving in endless ways and even without committing crimes of violence. In a way they brought together Kantian ethics and poetical longing. Perhaps no generation has ever achieved a finer standard of behaviour and culture. It could afford to eschew the 'blood of the Lamb' beliefs of atonement and with Goethe as a guide settle for its own type of reconciliation. Liberal theology issued from and spoke to this condition by drawing upon and misinterpreting Abelard's 'example of Christ'.

Even the Protestant work ethic could go along with Faust's salvation. The 'draining of the marshes' becomes almost a symbol of public works, carried out by a vast organisation led by the spirit of enterprise and sustained by effort. The more idealist theologian may see in this also the growth of new communities and the abolition of sickness and poverty. The social gospel flourishes on this tangible, this-worldly notion of atonement and tames the Faustian demonism to such an extent that one is liable to forget the pact with the devil. The slogans of progress unite with the clichés of the French revolution: equality, fraternity and liberty can be seen and felt, for example, in North America where the constitution enshrines ideals as if humans needed only good sense to leave behind the shadows of sin and guilt. If, however, a Calvinistic vocabulary or a Lutheran heritage remain in the bloodstream, then this basic conviction can still be reconciled with *sola gratia*, precisely the blessing of supernatural grace which Faust receives as the saving act.

But this best of all worlds, in which both Protestant and Catholic soteriology may seem to be satisfied, approached its collapse before 1914. As we have already seen, the outbreak of war deepened fissures in society and added even more searing wounds to the human psyche. It is tempting merely to look at pictures of trench warfare and to visit square miles of war cemeteries to collect evidence of the collapse of all idealism. But these pictures cannot convey to the onlooker the motivation which led the lambs to the slaughter and a whole educated civilisation to jump over the precipice into the despair of chaos. Faust, after all, according to Goethe, had been instrumental in preparing his own grave. Now the tomb received its victims in millions and still swallows them in ever increasing numbers.

No account can be given for the causes of the first world war. Thousands of books examine economic and political reasons and guilt is attributed to the Kaiser, the Czar, the Austrian intriguers, the capitalist cartels, French revanchism and English dithering. The list is endless. The fact remains that none of the actors on the stage of that history knew what would happen, least of all the military leaders! In retrospect French and Haig, Joffre and Foch, Hindenburg and Ludendorff and Sukhomlinov and Zhilinsky look ignorant though not innocent. Solzhenitsyn has chronicled with marvellous accuracy and insight the catastrophe that overtook the Russian armies in East Prussia in *August 1914*, but he does not stress sufficiently that their failures and disaster, due to criminally deficient leadership, happened to save the battle of the Marne and prevent the defeat of France.

These distant memories deserve to be revived when we

return to analyse the sinfulness of the beginnings of our apocalyptic age. No one concluded a pact with the devil, but the devil concluded his pact with the overweening *hubris* and the jubilant enthusiasm of the millions who welcomed war and therefore death. Here again documentation abounds in all European languages. Perhaps the most eloquent is Carl Zuckmayer's *'Als wärs ein Stück von mir'*, a verse snatched from the German soldiers' song *'Ich hatt'einen Kameraden'*. He describes how the young men, still at school and before their final examination, volunteered for service at the front. Were they guilty or innocent? What did they wish to escape from and what did they hope to find?

Theirs was a blending of boredom (ennui) and a readiness to die. For some reason the old world had come to bore the young. They longed for the Faustian adventure, and were soon to be disillusioned when it was too late. Here we have the perfect example of the free consent to corporate violence from sincere motives. And this time the devil did not lose the bet.

But the guilt could not be attributed to such a mythological figure as the devil. As millions mourned the deaths and as plague and famine tormented the survivors, the question 'Who was guilty?' was raised not only by the victims but also among the peace-makers. The Treaty of Versailles left no party in doubt that Germany was guilty and that reparations were to be exacted. The old theological equation was still operative in a wholly secular context. Guilt was never defined. The term presupposed that a nation or a geographical unit could be identified as a culprit and that it could be made to pay.

What follows is history. Reparations were not paid because they could not be paid. Instead money was printed, inflation started, armies of occupation moved into the Rhineland and the Ruhr, and Goethe's *Faust* was re-enacted on the corporate stage, with all its absurdity and uselessness. Meanwhile the devilish plot succeeded in the absence of real reconciliation. Millions lost all their savings and became an embattled minority, resistant to reconciliation and ready for extreme measures in the future. While the roaring twenties brought fame and fortune to a few and soon altered the balance of power, with the advent of the major Marxist state, the seed of further slaughter took root.

The political and the military aspect as well as the economic base for the new confrontation are better known than the spiritual reasons for it. Clearly, the war had killed idealism and the Christian influence was ebbing. In their way the German professors and theologians who had supported the war had pronounced the death sentence on the Church. But the Faustian morality, too, could not survive such a catastrophe. Salvation by genuine striving was discredited and was succeeded by a wave of nihilism. The gamble between mankind and its controlling destiny entered a new spiritual phase.

Christians seem to be too good-natured to come to terms with the devil, although, as we shall see, the New Testament concentrates on the meaning of the struggle on every level of experience. But the work of Christ as seen by most Christian theologians seems to spell Atonement and reconciliation even behind the worst excesses. Universal restoration and the love of God bring even Judas, i.e. traitors and desperate men, into the fold. Thus, surprisingly, even Karl Barth flirts with Origen's *apokatastasis*[1]. To all this we must return later.

In our century of unprecedented evil such sham solutions repel. But only rare spirits explore the spiritual dimension of deliberate and cruel nihilism. Some writers merely portray it, even to their own advantage, in sensational plays and films; others paint scenes of brutal horror. But the entertainment value of concentration camps is soon apprehended as another aspect of the devil's pact with the media and with corrupt minds. Behind all these stands the sober evidence in pictures and narratives of deeds done by men and women which torture the soul of mankind. Gone is the cynical playfulness of Goethe's Mephistopheles or the demonic heroism of Mozart's Don Giovanni. Rather the stage is held by Shakespearean villains, the offspring sired by the Iagos of every class and nation, the Macbeths of every *apparatchik*, the Claudiuses of endless administrators of death factories and so on. Nor do we fail to meet the Regans and Gonerils in Hitler's extermination camps and in Stalin's Gulags. Perhaps only the victims, the Bonhoeffers, the Edith Steins and the Ossip Mandelstamms (if these plurals may be allowed), have the right to comment on the spiritual nature of devilish inspiration and deeds.

Yet even these heroes and martyrs still valued Goethe's *Faust* although clearly neither this work of genius nor the popular legend can sustain the weight of our monstrosities. Many works about Faust have been written since Goethe's time, not to mention the musical rendering (Gounod) and snatches of Faust motifs. Goebbels, Hitler's mentor, may well have digested Faust under the guidance of his master, the Jewish professor Gundolf, and he almost seems in a perverse way to have opted to act the part of the devil. But few of the other villains would have been acquainted with the tradition since they cultivated their ignorance and, like Goering, wanted to shit upon culture (which did not prevent Goering from stealing great and valuable paintings).

Even so, another attempt with a grand design was made to interpret the German and European tragedy in the terms of the wager and the Faustian contempt of the consequences of losing the battle with the forces of hell. Thomas Mann began his monumental *Doctor Faustus* in California and completed the work at the end of the so-called second world war, i.e. in knowledge of the atrocities which stained the continent of Europe. He had already in *The Magic Mountain* explored the spiritual dimension of the sickness which led to the first world war, but his new sequence was not a repetition of the same theme. Whereas boredom, ennui and stupidity had allowed the slide into the first carnage, the second scene of total and insane murdering challenged the writer to scale unknown heights and depths. Mann left us a full description of the genesis of his work. In it he traces his personal movements, his resistance to tyranny, and the flow of events preceding the final defeat of the enemy.

But the political and the military elements are only

peripheral in Mann's *Doctor Faustus*. Indeed, the 'hero' of the novel is by no means the energetic and exploring captain of industry or political bully who could have filled the role of the modern magician. This Faustus, on the contrary, is an artist, a musician, a composer, delicate in health, but ruthless in the search for the perfect. Mann certainly did not create this *Leverkühn* as an emblem of Nazi barbarism or traditional German efficiency and militarism. The boy comes from peasant stock of an almost medieval and rural simplicity. His friend, the Catholic humanist Serenus Zeitblom, the alleged author of the memoir, describes in great detail this strange background of healthy and natural conditions mixed up with a search for the secrets of the universe, as reflected in the world of crystals and organic creatures. A good deal of suspect mysticism surrounds young Adrian. He becomes a student of theology. Fanaticism, sectarianism and all kinds of utopia entice the interest of the budding genius. Mann's picture of university life does not include the usual extravagances of youth, though drinking and brothels play their part; nor are magical tricks the landmarks of the narrative. This Faustus descends to a deeper level when he leaves theology and speculations. Musical and artistic tensions, modulations, hopes, despairs, corruptions and lusts initiate the pact with demonic ecstasy. Inspiration in the conventional sense is not in question here. Rather all the enthusiastic arrogance of the past, together with all the suffering involved in the ordeal of self-transcendence, culminate in a Nietzschean superman. Doctor Faustus, threatened by syphilis, sacrifices himself to the inner temptation of abandoning all ties, all affection, every obligation, in order to create the new, the unprecedented, the polyphony of serial music. This is certainly not the music of the Nazis; far from it! Nor could it ever be identified with Marxist-Leninist socialist realism. Yet *Leverkühn's* surrender of the soul renews the Faustian drive, the urge to divinise self or at least the work of self. Could this be an atoning sacrifice?

If suffering were the criterion of an acceptable sacrifice, then Adrian, the new Faustus, would fulfil his part. All the tragic convulsions of the past, in Greek mythology and in biblical lore, reappear in the modern artist, who wrestles with destiny to transcend the meaningless meanness of art and of life. Mann lightens the context by placing his Faustus in ridiculous circumstances. The tragic element is enhanced by the staging of the comedy of manners which auxiliary characters contribute. All the absurdities of their actions, prejudices, ambitions and expectations serve to isolate Faustus from the world in which he lives. He stands for the German spirit at its purest, its loneliest and its most perilous. Once, towards the end of the book, the spark of affection is struck by the company of his nephew, a little boy, nicknamed Echo. When Echo dies, without being spared the torments of meningitis and the attentions of doctors, Adrian reaches a point of no return from hell. The lamentations of Faustus and the apocalypse together fix the curse which he pronounces on all goodness; he cancels, he takes back and thus enters the void. Like Nietzsche he lapses into the stupor of insanity, a sacrifice to the demon that has possessed him. Thus the saga reaches a terrible end, for Mann, the worshipper of Goethe, cancels thereby the redemption of Faustus. There are no angels, no apostles, no saints, no penitents, no Mary, no bliss. The striving has been worse than in vain – a heroic oblation of self to self – and there is no reconciliation in the cosmos. Shakespeare's *Love's Labour's Lost* governs everything: loss remains the key. Denial, absurdity, bankruptcy and the void lead into despair.

The devils

As long as the demonic is located outside individuals and society, both individuals and society may be considered to be curable. The ordinary Christian approach to both has always been down-to-earth, offering reconciliation as a reasonable and desirable way out of strife. But this therapeutic optimism has already been seen to fail when reflected in the Faustian drama. The striving superman can either be redeemed after death, as with Goethe, or he fails completely because of his striving and falls into insanity.

Far less complicated and really quite straightforward is the perdition of men and societies which have been invaded by demonic forces and have become demonic themselves. In the New Testament, it is true, these enemies of humanity are treated by Jesus in a specific manner. The possessed are not healed in the ordinary way but they are separated from the evil within. This act of separation is carried out by command. The term 'exorcism' briefly summarises the dramatic encounter with the Lord who orders the expulsion. The possessed, who was beyond control, is left in a restored state of sanity. He can go home. He is reconciled to himself, to his family, to the community and to God. The simplicity of the act excludes sophisticated details, such as contrition or conditions of any kind. The demoniac is the recipient without further intermediary or special sacrifice. No blood is shed, though an act of transference seems to be involved, as if the spiritual had to perish in the physical. Legion, the unclean spirit, enters the swine, and the swine rush over the cliff into the lake where they drown.

The post-religious age does not accept this procedure, even though it may be effective in a number of cases which remain unexplained. Ever since the European spirit expanded, the demonic has not been separable from the character of individuals and society. For Dante, Muhammed was a devilish fraud because this was what he wanted to be. Indeed, all the foul creatures are what they are though they could have been different. The same may be said of social phenomena. Wars are the outcome of demonic possession and occur because the demonic has its own force.

Yet a total determinism also fails to take account of reality. If it were not so, i.e. if the element of freedom were not conspicuous, no dramatic climax could be attached to great tragic events. The huge tension between demonic force and human free will plays its part both in reality and on the stage. The tragedy of Macbeth is a tragedy because, following Shakespeare, the general returning with Banquo from battle could have resisted the witches' enticements, his wife's bloody ambition and his own devilish intent. The demonic only becomes Macbeth when the evil deed is done and steeped in blood he will not and cannot quit.

Most authors dealing with individuals pinpoint a dual nature in man, something like the good and the evil inclination of biblical tradition. But this attractive balance has a grim flaw, inasmuch as once the demonic has entered, like poison, no therapy is in sight. The spectacle among psychotic patients confirms what such extreme narratives as Stevenson's *Dr Jekyll and Mr Hyde* portray: the drug addict must murder in an orgy of violence. Like a lesser Faust he is lost in his liberated self. He has become a devil.

The mystery of evil cannot be resolved simply by opting for either total freedom or determinism. No one allows more profoundly for this tension than Dostoevsky. No doubt he knew what it meant to be 'possessed', to meet with the 'possessed' and to describe the punishment of the 'possessed'. Yet he also retains the longing for healing and redemption. Thus he prefaces the motto to the novel *The Devils* with the narrative of the healing of the demoniac, as given in Luke 8: 32–7. The emphasis here is on the transference of the demonic into the herd of swine which drown in the lake and on the spectacle of the cured patient now dressed and restored to rationality. The spectators, according to this narrative, are terrified. Dostoevsky also quotes from Pushkin lines about a party lost in the blizzard and torn about by demons – a vision of chaos.

The unique status of *The Devils* is undisputed. No one outside the New Testament has been able to correlate individual guilt, crime and sickness with corporate and cosmic evil as does Dostoevsky, who reflects the social-political nihilism and terrorism in individual characters and named personalities. The story rests upon the long Russian tradition of *RASKOL*, the struggle of the people involved in schism and fanaticism. A utopian apocalypse is the spiritual seedbed of brotherhoods, united in groups which could be mystically patriotic or revolutionary. These people, drawn from all classes of society, believed in violence as a principle. Ideas and actions brought together idealists and criminals. The earth was pregnant with 'new things' and the birth pangs could only be full of pain. Rebellion as an idea must be implemented in strikes and arson. Years before the outbreak of Marxist-led revolutions (in 1905 and 1917) and brutal civil war the agitprop machine was at work. Not peace but war, not order but anarchy, were aims pursued by militant atheists. Dostoevsky disclosed motivation and aims of a spiritual dimension. Both remain with us, powerful and unatoned.

In cells of five the conspirators organise a vast network. After the failure of the conspiracy one of them (Lamshin) makes a full confession which is not forced out of him. He enjoys the disclosure. Groups of members found new disciples and probe the weak spots in the established order. Asked why so many people were murdered and raped and why other crimes, such as the burning down of a whole quarter of factories and residences, were committed, he replies with persuasive logic that these actions were directed towards the systematic shaking of the foundations of society. If the scheme had worked, the sick and cynical mass of infidels would have rallied to the socialist utopia.

Cunning though Lamshin and his fellow conspirators were, they became tools in the hands of higher and better-educated planners. Lamshin confessed because he believed that the highest of them all, Stavrogin, would intervene on his behalf instead of making good his flight to Switzerland. All the conspirators bring different resentments to their cause, but envy and fear are common to them. The image is that of a spider's web in which the flies are caught. They work together within the web without trusting one another. Having surrendered freely to this common bond their freedom perishes altogether, unless they see from within that they are being manipulated. Then even a conspirator may turn away in moral disgust, and by desiring to relinquish membership becomes the target of the circle. Shatov is such a one who will no longer act as a wolf and thus becomes a sacrificial lamb. His death is the theological climax of the novel. Far from being outwardly attractive and having a rotten past, he is the modern equivalent of the demoniac; restored and rational through suffering and death. The rest are caught, tried and punished. But the mysterious Lucifer, Stavrogin, the son and heir of a general and a rich mother, hangs himself in an attic in the canton of Uri. Life, he declares in a final summary, has become ridiculous and nauseating. Love might have saved him, but he has excluded himself from love in the terrible flatness of debauchery and revolutionary antics.

Dostoevsky was not content to write a political tract. If he had done so the whole story would have been predictable and one-sided. For example, the progenitor of the arch-villain, Pyotr Verkovensky, who is the liberal, kind and lazy father, Stephan, is at first simply a client of a rich benefactress, the mother of Stavrogin. Stephan prefers to mouth French clichés in place of Russian utterances; he is wholly pretentious, affected and pedantic, a victim of conceit and sentimentality. But this theatrical humbug is seen to be directly responsible for a murderous son whose lack of moral scruple must be attributed to his having been neglected as a child. In short, the equation fatuous liberalism equals calculating brutality seems to pervade the whole analysis of corporate guilt. But, surprisingly, at the end of the novel Stephan abandons shelter and privilege and (almost prefiguring the death of Tolstoy) dies as a Christian. He repents and (unlike Tolstoy) receives the sacrament. He does not fall into the pit which he had helped to dig.

Thus suffering and death seal repentance for those who have eyes to see and ears to hear. The catastrophe which overtakes the community by fire is also turned to good account among the few of 'good society' who can stand outside their own vanity. The comedy of 'do-gooders' whose charity ball is the prelude to the fire comes to act as an apocalyptic warning of judgment. The devils cannot be placated by fashionable social events; only a clear apprehension of real forces can expose their intentions.

Over a hundred years have passed since this novel was given to the world. Nothing has changed except that now the devils are in power and their revolution has become institutionalised. Supported by the control of the media and military force, the godless authority rules and darkness covers the world.

Christians can become involved in deadly sin when they wish to extend the Atonement of Christ to the perpetrators of unrepented evil. The physical and spiritual evils are worse than the words which describe them. The accounts, even of Solzhenitsyn, enable us to stand apart from Gulag atrocities and to close the book, but the book of judgment cannot so lightly be closed, and all our moral instincts are outraged if the pardon of devils and devilry is envisaged as a Christian virtue. The pathology of cruelty cannot deflect attention from the systematic promotion of the spiritual evil. De Sade can be viewed as a case of madness, just as the latest case of child-beating and torturing may be assigned to the files of medical analysis. This is not so with the never-ending machinery which finds its sole *raison d'être* in the administration of death.

Origen, therefore, and all his followers must be refuted, and the suicides of the criminals must expose their despair. Even if in Gestapo and KGB annals the suicides are rare and the material rewards seem to point to the opposite, the deaths of the tormentors do at length vindicate the truth. How they will fare in eternity is not for man to declare, but the Christian conception of the judgment extends into eternity. There the deaths of the righteous blend with the stars in the most blessed light.

When the devil was merely a folk hero with horns and tail, or a dragon-like figure with a Satanic name such as Beelzebub or Lucifer, such an infernal ruler of darkness could be contained in our mental scaffold. He was outside, just as the shadow we cast is outside. This has changed, for the devils now confront us from within as well as from above, hostile and powerful forces outside our control.

Measure for Measure

To leave behind the stench of metaphysical pollution and to go on living as if traitors, murderers, panderers, seducers and torturers were not in our midst and working away in their organisations, is itself evidence of the grace of God and its atoning power in the human soul. Peace, joy and love seem so remote from the cesspool of damnation that, like Dante and Virgil, we breathe again when we see the stars. No prosaic statement can express the relief from seeing, hearing and smelling the fetid horror. But we do not take flight from the reign of terror when we give thanks for our own reconciliation.

How can it be achieved? How can the hand of God be clasped by the guilty? Our own sense of justice decrees that guilt must be met by forgiveness. The image of the balance arises before our eyes. Though we cannot hope to present the weights to balance our misdeeds we can apply a sense of proportion to the imbalance. Here we switch from poetry to prose, for we need a cool assessment of qualities and quantities, yardsticks to measure the enormities as well as the trivialities of our offences. But the calculations required often defeat us, for how can we register the qualities of committed sins? The ancient world provided, both in Israel and outside, a scale by which they could be weighed. Thus an almost arithmetical principle was in operation and a sum of the debt fixed. This could be paid in all kinds of sacrifices or even in silver money. Compensation was a welcome means of settling the debt.

This principle still held its validity until the sixteenth century, and among the Jews until the Holocaust in eastern Europe. Professionals among lawyers, priests and rabbis were trained to compound justice with mercy, for they did not ignore special circumstances in the breach of the laws. The question could still be asked not only why a sin was committed but also with what degree of severity and how often. Thus categories of quality and quantity were by no means meaningless. For example, a single curse or blasphemy was not as bad as a repeated utterance against God and the king. Inquisitors were even able to divorce the sin from the sinner, by forgiving the latter upon repentance without condoning the deed. Famous examples of this procedure are known, but they are now generally looked upon with a smile and even contempt. Thus Shaw's St Joan is offered conditions for a pardon which in the end she cannot accept. Life-long imprisonment seems to her worse than death, and a recantation not worth the dishonour. A certain amount of plea-bargaining always existed in fixing a penalty and could discredit the machinery of justice even then. However, the system worked for most people and especially for those who were sinners without being criminals. They would confess their sins, receive absolution, do penance and thus become eligible for God's free pardon, especially after death. The human transaction could always be seen in perspective, namely for Christians as the result of the work of Christ.

The Reformation, however, brought to a head protest and dissatisfaction. Too much money was being extorted in the human transaction, and Luther had only to denounce the sale of indulgences to succeed not only in northern Europe but also indirectly in loyal Catholic regions. Forgiveness could no longer be for sale, and it is not for sale now. What then can take its place? If payment cannot be fixed, what other measures can be used to assess serious and not-so-serious sins and to make things right for the offended and the offenders?

Matters are complicated enough in law, both civil and criminal. But at least all parties believe that actions and offences can be appraised rationally, even if this procedure does not often lead to reconciliation. Punishment, for example, is mainly devised to deter future evil-doers and to protect the community. Retribution is out of favour. Attempts to legislate for compensation often fail altogether, if only because the guilty party cannot or will not pay. But throughout there is no pretence that the former state of innocence can be obtained.

The non-legalistic approach transcends the merely juridicial goal, for it looks not only at deeds but at doers. The relationship between people is at stake, and it affects the community. Hence one may almost despair of finding a method of establishing any kind of procedure to make for peace after war, for concord after discord. The Christian carries the added burden that Christ must somehow stand at the centre of any reconciliation for it to be genuine. It is through the Holy Spirit that forgiveness can be desired and received. This dimension seems to go beyond all reasonable limits of appraising measures for measures, but according to the claims of the Judaeo-Christian tradition the cosmic, transcendent spiritual alone achieves the desired end. Nor is this claim as fantastic or romantic as it may sound, for we have seen, especially in the present century, that all moral standards, and therefore all judgments, can vanish in the quicksands of relativism. Without a transcendental reference there is no categorical imperative, no definition of justice and the good. It is enough to be told that what is considered an offence in the west may be acclaimed a virtue in the east (e.g. various types of sexual conduct, attitudes towards marriage, neglect of widows, exposure of infants) and all 'measuring' becomes a nonsense.

Given the firm stance of revealed and of rational morality, such a relativistic vanishing trick can be countered. But the enormous complexity remains and, let it be said, it adds to the enjoyment of the whole subject of reconciliation.

There are no mechanics to work the balances. A subtle weighing-up outside the machinery attracts the genius of mankind. Shakespeare presents us with the supreme drama in many plays, but nowhere more directly than in the problem play *Measure for Measure*. When I lectured for a whole term on the Atonement to theological students this play was the text on which to draw. It gives an extreme case which could make bad law, but does not. It could also sentimentalise mercy to discredit it, but does not. Shakespeare orchestrates a polyphonic dispute which hovers between the extremes of tragedy and comedy. Hence no one ever gets to the bottom of this play; whenever one returns to read or see it a new element of substance is perceived.

The plot seems simple enough, taken from Cinzio's *Ecatommiti*. The Duke appoints his severe deputy to take his place during his absence: 'Lord Angelo is precise'. But this Angelo whose task it is to end fornication and immorality turns out to be less 'bloodless' than he seemed to the Duke and perhaps to himself. Having condemned Claudio for begetting a child before marriage, he lusts after Isabella, Claudio's sister. This lust soon grows into something far worse, for Angelo demands Isabella's virginity in exchange for sparing Claudio's life. But behind this 'measure for measure' lurks his determination to win the girl, a pious novice nun, by blackmail and then not to keep to the bargain. In the confusion of brothels and prisons Angelo hands down the order for Claudio's execution. The moralist has become blackmailer, would-be seducer and murderer.

So far the plot seems to raise no legal or moral problem. Angelo is simply a villain who ought to be punished. The only question is whether intended murder is the same as murder itself. There must also be some doubt about the judge himself, for the Duke, acting in this capacity, may be deemed to have been guilty as an accessory. He started the whole thing and by testing the deputy also led him into temptation. Nor is this all, for the Duke punishes one Lucio, the ribald, prattling, salacious libertine who started the rescue of Claudio by informing Isabella of her brother's evil fate. His sin appears to be no more than speaking gossiping innuendoes against the Duke when he was disguised as a friar.

But the problems lie deeper than these somewhat comic points and really concern atonement. Some producers of the play ignore the spiritual content, but then the play fails for them. No producer can evade the problem of the Duke's character: does he act as a virtuous ruler, a representative of divine justice, acting like God? Or is he the accuser of mankind, like Satan? Does he mean what he says, as when he recommends death as the best way to life? Or does he merely seem to be just and good?

The play opens the way to reconciliation not only because the Duke prevents the catastrophe which Angelo desired to bring about. Claudio is not executed, Isabella is not violated. Instead Mariana meets Angelo at night in bed; the bed-trick, a comic device, works well enough. But Angelo neither deserves nor desires atonement; rather he pleads for 'immediate sentence and then death'. He craves death more willingly than mercy. His trouble is emotional and spiritual; he cannot repent.

His repentance would make impossible demands upon his personality and he is too intelligent to ignore the total loss of face he would suffer. He has failed at every level. Once again we meet a cheater who is found out and is therefore cheated of everything. But does he deserve to be spared? Could he be restored? Shakespeare does not tell us, but he allows Mariana to love him, and at her request Isabella intercedes for Angelo. Having been the main target of his treacherous lechery she can afford to take his part. This is saintly behaviour, an unthinkable ideal outside the whole Christian edifice of atonement in which the sacrifice of Christ pleads for the lost. Love for the unlovable transcends the merely erotic desire.

This play almost denies the validity of its own title and continues to challenge legal and religious principles. We have seen that reconciliation without 'measure' is unobtainable, whether it be in public or private areas of conflict. But once the intercessory action is included in such 'measure' we move on a plane beyond ordinary methods of compensation. In today's terms awards of millions of dollars are paid for injuries and torts; thus claims are settled or fail to be settled. But even today the spiritual pain after genocide, exile or divorce cannot be annulled by payments of any kind. Only pure goodness, offering itself freely, can erase the wounds of the past, even if scars remain. The modern Angelo may be restored, not out of penitence but into penitence, by something or some intercessors beyond and above him. *Measure for Measure* therefore gives a mystical weight in the realistic task of balancing the books. This substitution of one thing by another is at the heart of Christian feeling and hope.

And yet it would be a mistake to forgo the notion of all measures, even to the point of qualities and quantities. It does matter whether we deal with accidental homicides, for example, or with planned and cruel murders. Even the intention alone cannot be measured without its consequence. Dostoevsky stresses this point in *Crime and Punishment*, when the murderer Raskolnikov murders not only the old usurer but also her sister, contrary to all his plans. His guilt, needless to say, precedes the action, for in his alienated isolation and resentment this student of law had already dreamt up his role as Napoleon, for whom 'all things are permitted'. But his calculation fails not only because all things are *not* permitted but because his double murder exposes the futility of his plans.

Raskolnikov typifies the problem of reconciliation. On the one hand it is solved by the criminal's idiocy, which is possibly not representative of murderers and robbers. Raskolnikov almost forgets to pick up the hidden booty. But this alone is no step nearer reconciliation. His pangs of conscience are almost muted by his condition. Nevertheless, as the detective anticipates, this type of criminal will not evade justice for long. He will seek his own arrest and trial. All the same, the punishment, even if looked at as retribution, does not revive the dead victims or atone for the deed. Again the old questions confront the criminal, or rather the author and the reader: How can penitence be infused? Can there be a change of heart?

Here again the intercession of a woman 'saves the soul'.

Sonja, who gives her body as a prostitute to feed the starving family, sacrifices her soul by befriending, loving and following her man into exile. The climax of her intercession comes with the reading of the raising of Lazarus from the dead. The Gospel confronts the murderer in the most unromantic and unpromising manner. There is no sudden conversion. Penitence comes as a very slow growth and even the final outcome is not certain.

The trial

Apart from attending a performance of *Measure for Measure*, the best introduction for people without a religious awareness to the complexities of atonement is to act as a juror or be a spectator at a trial in the law courts. Centuries have passed and procedures have altered, but the heart of the matter is the same: the search for justice. Perverted justice is a constant threat and was not unknown in antiquity. Judges and witnesses may be bribed and tyrants may dispense with all forms of justice. Again rough justice may be carried out as in primitive vendetta which also continues to claim its victims to this day. But abuses do not abrogate the proper uses, indeed the abuses have been the causes of establishing impartial justice. Without bias or favour and disregarding influence and wealth, justice must be seen to prevail, and in order to arrive at such an ideal an orderly procedure must be followed.

The purpose of trials varies, and accordingly we distinguish between civil and criminal cases. This compartmentalisation obscures only too often the undefined aim of manifesting the truth and achieving reconciliation on the basis of truth. Common law has become too pragmatic to serve such an ideal. But even the accumulation of laws, as handed down in the Bible, never disguises the practical goal. Conditions are specified: if this or that has happened then the appropriate penalty will apply. The events which call for reparation are as diverse as life itself. Life can be polluted by neglect of ceremonies and ritual, even if unwittingly committed; trespasses and torts disturb the community; crimes cry out for vengeance. Thus trials may embrace matters which western courts would now consider irrelevant. We no longer accuse people of immoral behaviour, or charge them with blasphemy and ritual offences.

Endless are the documents from the ancient Near East which articulate protestations of innocence. These protestations were not only made use of in cases brought before a court but, more significantly, were also used before such cases occurred. They may have been looked upon as a kind of prophylactic. Kings and leaders were expected to declare their innocence before they could be acclaimed. But the search for acquittal probably went much further in certain cases. One of David's psalms begins with the question: 'Lord, who shall dwell in thy tabernacle?' and goes on to answer in terms of perfect equity. Walking uprightly, working righteousness and speaking the truth are the positive virtues; not slandering, not doing evil, not deceiving the neighbours are negative promises. The immovable just man stands before God and the community. Psalm 15 thus briefly summarises the expectation, the norm, the ideal without which no one can rule or be ruled. But if the cause of the righteous stands in danger or is lost, the psalmists (David and his successors) call for God to stand by them in their just cause. This *RIV* is a sacred cause which becomes a matter of strife and dispute, for the righteous battles against the enemy. In this controversy between herdsmen, neighbours, peoples, nations, man pleads and conducts his case unaided by the law. He calls upon God to plead for him (Ps. 35) and take his part.

The business of intercession and substitution really begins with these heart-rending pleas. They are uttered on behalf of the suffering community, Zion, the righteous, the remnant, the solitary prophet. In the psalms the agony precedes the resolution. The trial ends with succour. But what happens when God is on the other side? Then a tragic dimension opens up in which innocence lacks vindication and the righteous suffers, being wrongly condemned. The unwilling martyr takes his stand with Job in the Bible, and with the unnamed K. in Kafka's *The Trial*.

For Job and his successors reconciliation is an ideal which becomes less accessible and more remote as the complex problem unfolds. If Job were merely attacked by the enemy, the Satan, he would, like all the martyrs, have to wait for a turn of events or die in hope. But neither prospect opens a solution, for Job's trial only begins with loss of property and incurable disease. Under the weight of the 'friends' presence and their arguments, the perspective shifts totally. In rebutting the charge that he has sinned and stands in need of forgiveness, Job eliminates the time-honoured procedures of getting right with God and the world. Instead he distances himself from the common lot of men and dwells upon his former state of royal independence; he has been everything that the protestations of innocence had laid down as a norm of perfection. He had been feet to the lame and eyes to the blind. He had also not broken any law, be it of ceremonial or family piety. The 'friends' may condemn him and seek a chink in his armour in view of his state as an outcast, but their moralising merely enforces Job's conviction that it is the moral law, or rather the law-giver, who wounds, hunts, torments and humiliates the innocent. Job's trial is the trial of one who can neither identify the accusation against him, nor the accusers, nor the judge. Accordingly he concludes that God himself is the enemy and spurred on by his interlocutors he reverses the situation; he is not on trial, but God is on trial. He even universalises his case. Though his claims to perfection may be exceptional he also represents mankind. The ordeal of life is inescapable as the sparks fly upward! There is hope even for a fallen tree, but there is no hope for man who is bullied by superior power beyond his reach.

Job's rhetoric is self-sustaining and grows sharper in its radical demands. Confrontation with God is sought as the only possible answer. Job disdains therapy or any compromise. Clearly it is now up to God to reconcile himself with Job. Let God make atonement and cover the pollution of injustice! Some next-of-kin will avenge Job, stand by his side, leap over the wall of total corruption, extend the vision and mysteriously bring to an end the intolerable destiny. Nor will this be an impersonal event, a sort of decision given by a remote court. On the contrary, at long last the I, the myself, the buffeted and tortured I, will see, behold, contemplate . . .: none other than God himself, no longer the enemy but the total satisfaction beyond life and death. The redeemer has mediated the impossible. The inaccessible wisdom which conceals God and the cosmic mantle which reveals God ensure the eternal validity of Job's trial of God. In view of these transcendent truths, which stand beyond all 'measure', even Job may submit.

One is almost inclined to ignore the extraordinary reversal that has taken place. For centuries commentators simply refused to come to terms with it. Accordingly both God and Job seemed justified, the former by his great speech out of the whirlwind and the final restoration of Job, the latter by his patience and submission. Thus Job himself became institutionalised and canonised. Yet the text never ceased to hit back against this conventional truce, and when the industrial age began Job became the representative of the isolated and alienated individual, great in potential but miserable in fact. When Blake identified with Job and portrayed him in unforgettable forms, not only did the rebel re-emerge, but also a strange God. God and Job had become one. The atonement without sacrament was given to the world in verse and form.

How, then, does Blake's Job attain to peace after war? According to himself the whole business of man is the arts and all things common. The perishing mortal eye can and must perceive through the imagination; spirit and vision save man from Jobian alienation. The infirmity of the imagination has allowed him to lose the divine integrity which is his; this can now be regained in self-revelation. The inward eye commands the centre of reality. By asserting his own version of neo-Platonic, cabbalistic and Swedenborgian symbols, Blake recasts the proper focus of atonement; not without Christ, but certainly without Christian soteriology. In this he follows Milton. Ambiguities and inconsistencies are part of this type of atonement, but they by no means delete suffering which achieves the paradise within. Jack Kahn in *Job's Illness* has given a psychological commentary tracing the course of the hero's illness, which derives from a disastrous neurosis, the search for complete perfection. The price for the release is really incalculable for it cannot be paid unless and until healing is willed and accepted.

For centuries, then, Job had stayed within religious tradition, i.e. of lamentation, prayer, penitence and acceptance. The modern age despairs of this message and refutes the notion of theodicy, the justification of God's ways to man. Modern commentaries go much further than Blake in updating Job. For example, the author is said to initiate the theatre of the absurd, as if Job were a character who turns tragic alienation into comedy. In a world of complete irrationality (as in Pinter and Beckett) the rational quest is the greatest fault. Reconciliation with the irrational and meaningless is possible . . . by scoffing laughter, a kind of defiance.

The trial ends with the verdict that there is no case to answer. But if we follow Blake and his innumerable champions not many people fulfil the conditions of self-salvation. By failing to stir their imagination and by cultivating a blindness and deafness of the senses they remain lost and separated. As Keats insisted, souls have to be 'made'; it is not an automatic process. Hence the optimism inherent in all the varieties of salvation by art can only be valid for the elect few. They are fortunate that they experience the ecstatic moment in which they are at one with the all. If they blend their experience with art they succeed in perpetuating the moment and perhaps in giving it to others. These claims are certainly substantially true when applied to the great western tradition. For example, the music of Monteverdi, Bach, Handel, Haydn, Mozart and Beethoven undoubtedly resolves and takes away sin and guilt. The creation becomes redemptive in the listener, just as a play on the stage communicates its mysterious power over the soul.

But the trial of man can also be made worse and more deadly by the imagination. It is the imagination which kindles the fire of brutality. Far from subscribing to the optimistic calculus, Jung gave an *Answer to Job* which outlines a frightening scenario. This Answer is also based upon psychological insight and upon the result of decades of reflection upon the problem of evil. Jung disdains the monotheistic approach and inverts the optimism of Blake. Jung also envisages a kind of therapy of the soul. The 'evil' is itself a transcendent fact, the Satan belongs to the divine society. Man's burden of atonement belongs to the collective unconscious and the individuation is the purpose of existence. All struggles, ordeals and trials derive from the dark reality which must and can be overcome. Grace and mercy stand against guilt and punishment. Job receives an answer which calls upon him to assist, redeem, pray for, God.

If Jung's Job receives a challenge to be God for God and thus to tame neurotic demonism – in God or in himself? – an even less promising search for peace and acceptance is granted to Kafka's hero, Josef K. His case takes the trial of man into the innermost recesses of consciousness and dreams. Like Job, Josef K. acts only by reacting. As he is arrested and loses his freedom in a comedy of idiotic questions and answers, he behaves like a child. But law is law and guilt is guilt. No error is possible. The guilty seeks his accusers, though the arrest comes as a surprise to him, for he considers himself innocent. The main question must clarify the nature of the charge and the authority of the accuser. Is the whole thing perhaps a game? Or a conspiracy by envious competitors? Suspicions are not evidence, unless sexual appetites, even if unknown to others and perhaps to oneself, even a kiss, may militate against one's purity.

Josef K. is no Job, except that he also concentrates in all he does on clearing himself and proving his innocence. In his machinations, contrivances and expedients he naturally outstrips Job, for he lives in the modern world of offices and bureaucracy. But the most formal interrogations have a fantastic aspect, which K. takes to be typical for all interviews which deal with liability and guilt. But what is the sense of judicial organisations? To accuse and convict the innocent who have to endure patiently the corrupt administration of a parody of justice? There is a way of defending oneself, but the accused is soon overcome by the tedium, the filth, the evil air. Fatigue and confusion overcome the best defendant. And in the dim outlines of almost invisible shadows there is sadistic torturing. But almost more painful are the lawyers, the files of paper, the false gleams of hope, the superficial acknowledgement by others that everyone must carry his cross. But two items remain hidden and unknowable: justice and judge.

Since there cannot be a proper trial, following a procedure in court, the anticipation of the trial becomes its proper definition. 'The thought of the trial never left him': hence Josef K. is eager to explain himself. His lawyer humiliates him, false trails are pursued, favourable signs point in the wrong direction, documents are secret and unobtainable for the defendant, progress is regress, appeals to a higher authority are of ambiguous value, and three forms of acquittal must be envisaged: real, apparent and procrastination. The verdict of 'not guilty' is only theoretically possible. In fact, a final acquittal will never be pronounced. Numerous paintings of the same blasted heath accompany pictorially these arid findings.

The famous scene in the cathedral completes the disaster. K. awaits an Italian businessman in the gloom of the building. The void and the darkness govern the stillness in which the priest calls for Josef K. It is the prison chaplain who confronts the accused. He tells him the story of the fur-capped porter and custodian of the law whose power has intimidated the man from the country. For many years the man craves admission to the law. Only when the doors are closed is he given to understand that this entrance was for him. The scripture does not lie, adds the priest; there was no deception, but Josef K. is not convinced. The priest insists that not everything has to be true; it must only be necessary. Then, concludes K., 'The lie becomes the order of the world'. He is dismissed with the opaque words that the court demands nothing of you; it accepts you when you come, and it releases you when you go. The last scene is brief: a ritualistic execution, but a shameful death as of a dog. Before his eyes break he sees a light in the distance; could this signify a friend, a compassionate arm which would help if it could? But there is no sign of the court and the judge. The trial ends in death.

III
VISIONS
OF
HEAVEN

Death and atonement

Reconciliation between parties is an ongoing process. On many levels quarrels and torts cause division, hatred and strife. Even if they stagnate and remain unresolved their consequences are often trivial and by no means world-shaking. But as soon as atonement appears as a desired and possible goal a matter of life and death confronts us. Ordinary mortality does not impinge on the issue; the fact that men are born and return to the dust, wither like the grass and fade like the flower, ceases to evoke the slightest attention. Only the tragic and undeserved and mostly violent death, which is an affront to nature and an outrage to our moral feelings, relates to atonement. Sickness and decay as stages towards dying have nothing to say in this context. The long lists of deaths in the papers, reports of accidents and of ghastly crimes, obituary notices in praise of the dead, even monuments erected to the fallen and cemeteries kept in memory of the departed, contribute nothing to our theme. These merely confirm what we have always known. Dying and death, mourning and separation, religious services with formal funeral rites, wreaths and donations and many natural consequences of death, such as wills and sales of property, merely tell the old story: you must die.

Nevertheless the passing from the visible and palpable

sphere of organic existence to the unknown opens the immense gulf between being and not-being. It seems inconceivable that a whole life with all its aspirations and achievements, its ordeals and unfulfilled longings, should be blotted out as if it had never been. Hence the affirmation of life implies a denial of death and the ending of life is felt to be hostile to the living. Death is proclaimed the enemy.

This enemy is not always recognised as such. On the contrary, death is often acclaimed as a welcome friend. Religious and irreligious people agree on death as a release from pain. True, the death of a child is terrible, but as the poet in Schubert's *Death and the Maiden* expresses the theme of consolation, death has not come to punish. Death is not the dreaded spectre of skull and bones and sickle, but the friend of the soul, liberated from physical strain and spiritual agony.

This gladness to get rid of the world, of striving and self and of physical torture, comes to a climax when we face intolerable conditions. The political prisoner has nothing to look forward to. Dietrich Bonhoeffer's brother Claus may be cited for millions as an example. He speaks for millions when he looks forward to his own execution. Having endured unbearable torture and resisted his torturers he is heard to long for the end; 'not to see those faces any more'. Like so many martyrs he has defeated the enemy by his death.

Even the death sentence pronounced by unrighteous judges may be transcended and death may be welcomed in a sophisticated manner. Socrates, whose last hours are described for us in the *Crito*, has become the unforgettable philosopher who drinks the hemlock with complete serenity and impresses jailer and friends with his total self-control. His ironical estimate of the judges and their proceedings does not lessen their guilt[1].

In their own way and unintentionally they have set Socrates on his way to a better future. In his famous statement he distinguishes between the perfect sleep which death may provide for him and the survival of his soul. If the latter is true, as he believes, the soul will find a reward for a virtuous life in a continuing identity. Socrates had always argued for the autonomy of the soul. After death the soul will be free and he will mingle among the great immortals. Such a confidence in an eternal destiny stands in no need of a mediating sacrifice.

These illustrious spirits are not concerned with sin as the very sting of death. The evils suffered as well as the injuries wittingly or unwittingly committed do not disturb them. A long line of heroic warriors, of artists and also of inarticulate simple folk pass from this life and expect the fulfilment of their wishes, of their very selves, in the bodiless future. Thus Shakespeare's 'golden lads and girls', untouched by the sting of a bad conscience, 'fear no more the heat o' the sun'. Goethe himself, not untouched by pangs of conscience, bears witness to the future hope. Though he hated the phenomenon of dying and would not 'see' death even in the shape of a funeral cortège in the street (funerals had to bypass his dwelling) he is convinced that the residual identity will achieve immortality. No atonement figures in his speech about the *entelechy*; as the caterpillar must become a butterfly so the essential self grows into eternal individuality.

The rub of the matter clearly derives from the experience of evil. Death in itself is not that evil. In the biblical tradition the patriarchs, for example, die a natural death, full of years. They are buried with care, setting an example to Israelite institutions regarding burials in the earth, dust to dust. After a full life the dead join their fathers. The intimacy of family life is not diminished by death.

Life after death by no means diminishes the sense of wrong endured and the thirst for vengeance. The heroes of Greek mythology do not rest in their graves. Hades is a place of terror and the underworld of punishment; Rhadamanthus judges the dead. There is no peace there for the wicked. But happiness is not even the lot of the less prominent, excluded as they are from Elysian delights.

The final state of the dead cannot be reduced to one common denominator in any culture. Both cheerful notions, as in Egypt, and anticipation of doom, as in Mesopotamia, influenced the Hebrews. Their underworld is one of shades and although there the wicked cease from troubling and the prisoner is at rest, survival brings no joy. This shadowy existence gave no comfort in times of great distress when the nation was assaulted from without, betrayed from within and the great misery of exile began. Then a longing for vindication that would yield blessing to the just and a curse to the unjust was felt at least among some. But this was not enough. Death, the fear of death, the horror of corpses, the memory of bleached skeletons on the battlefield, the tortures of God's servant, had to be put right. Death certainly did not deserve a welcome as a natural release nor could death itself pronounce the final verdict on nations and individuals. The slain would reassemble their limbs and sinews and yet being lifeless they would receive a new life in the spirit. Thus a mighty army of reborn martyrs would rise up, vindicated and glorious. Even if the world would count the victims as poor and defeated, they were in the hand of God. Thus evil and the horror of evil prepared a martyred community for a rising again, the resurrection.

Clearly this vast undertaking lies beyond the natural world. It demands the will to create a new dimension for the natural order. It cannot answer to the need unless death itself loses its power and sin is purged. But death as the end of life and the passage to another life remains the central pivot of all that has gone before. As in Kafka's *The Trial*, we confront a door, the gate to the secret of human destiny. Even modern atrocities on a huge scale and of monstrous cruelty cannot obscure this gate of eternal judgment.

Atonement as a possibility and as a goal completely alters the acceptable face of death. It annuls notions of simple negations. Even the most trivial life is now seen in the context of continuance, facing the either – or of judgment. Extinction would be desirable in many instances but atonement challenges nothingness, as if life could be reduced to zero. On the other hand, contrary to many religious speculations, it also militates against the transmigration of souls. If reincarnation could be proved there would be no further grounds for atonement. We should die and according to our deeds, intentions and relationships we should have to relive the past. The so-called *karma* would be dealt with by ourselves, whether we liked it or not. But this way of self-reconciliation after death is excluded by all levels of atonement, for they never agree with a circular return to the beginning based upon the end. The circle is a symbol of life – death – life which contradicts every Christian desire for atonement. Other symbols which mark the ascent of the soul will serve this end.

Sacrifice and atonement

In the world of animals the stronger may eat the weaker, but the stronger may also defend the helpless. Parents stand between the beasts of prey and their offspring. The mother bird fends off the killer, the male fights with his life for that of his mate. There appears to be no general rule in the immense diversity of struggling species which must eat and propagate. Instinctive needs prompt patterns of what seem to us unselfish acts of sacrifice. The same readiness to give a life for a life continues to operate in humans. It is not even considered to be a particular virtue and many a parent would echo David's cry 'Would that I had died for thee!'. The pleasure principle which governs so much of life gives way to a principle of sacrifice. It aims at preserving and promoting the wellbeing and continuance of the family unit. This unit is widened into larger circles of clans and tribes until nations displace these and are swallowed up into even greater collectives. But the principle of sacrifice survives the loss of intimacy, so that the members of the community can be expected to give something of themselves, even their lives, in instances of need. This instinct for sacrifice flourishes in conflicts and wars, but it is also a notable factor in maintaining and restoring unity. Hence the search for atonement relies upon the availability of sacrifice, the willingness of those able to act to come between the threatened and their enemies. When no such interceding power can be found all is lost and death must win. Kafka's Josef K. looks in vain for help outside himself, prefiguring the terrible sight of trucks of Jews being carried off, in worse conditions than cattle, to be gassed and burned.

Self-sacrifice for high principles can proceed from flawed characters and wounded pride. Antigone defies her uncle Creon and buries her dead brother in the full knowledge that she will die for her heroic gesture. Tragic self-sacrifice purges our emotions with pity, but it cannot atone for past and present terrors. Looking back we are moved by the sacrifice of millions of lives in what now appear to be unworthy causes. After Napoleon's and Hitler's wars we feel a cynical revulsion against the false ideals of sacrifice. In 1945 mere boys fought needlessly to 'the bitter end'. The first world war had created in England an opposition to heroism, and the war cemeteries were interpreted by many as memorials to wasted lives[1].

Religious sacrifices may be even worse, but they point to a deep need to placate forces beyond human control. The practice of human sacrifice seems in some parts of the world to be as ancient as the human race. Whole burnt offerings or holocausts would be offered to pay homage to the high god. Not only were captives immolated on altars but the blood of children was shed.

The sacrifice of Iphigenia stands out as a classical example. Here the priest demands of the father a precious victim so that the wind may change and the fleet may sail on against Troy. In Judges 11 we listen to a similar story; Jephtha's daughter must die since her father offered 'whoever comes forth of the doors of my house to meet me' when he prayed to obtain a favourable outcome to battle.

The most poignant narrative concerns the Binding of Isaac, *Aqedah* in Genesis 22. Abraham was ordered to offer up his son Isaac. The walk of father and son to Mt Moriah until the question is asked: 'Where is the lamb for a burnt offering?' confronts the listener with the *tremendum et fascinans* of sacrifice. Generations of scholars and mystics have meditated upon the story. How can a good God command a father to draw the knife to kill his son, a son of promise? But the order was never carried out; the angel interfered at the last moment. Abraham had been tested, the victim is spared. The slaughter of the lamb and the injunction to obey God take the place of infanticide. Substitution and obedience, not murder, are the real sacrifice.

The sacrificial cultus in Israel disdains human sacrifice and develops the sacrifice of animals. To the rational and enlightened sceptic of our western world the sacrificial cultus must seem incomprehensible. However, when he turns to look at the unenlightened and perhaps to the pathological, the dark world of slaughter and blood, he may stop to reflect.

Not all sacrificial rites are intended for reconciliation with man or the deity. Offerings are made for fertility, each season having its appropriate form of oblation or libation. Social gatherings enter into communion by sharing a sacrificial meal; families through their representatives give thanks for benefits or implore aid by giving presents. Peace offerings and sin offerings are available when strife separates neighbours or damages call for compensation. Even in the Israel of Judaism money can change hands instead of animals, vegetables or fruit. But none of these occasional rituals touches directly on atonement, though they stabilise the social fabric. However, the law of compensation has close points of contact with atoning sacrifices, and no atonement can be effected apart from sacrifice.

The world of the ancient Near East, not to mention other cultures, had the widest range of sacrifices. Among the Hebrews sacrifice vanished from the countryside, the villages and the local high places. Whereas elsewhere, as in Italy, the lesser gods received their tribute in the home, the prophetic movement outlawed 'paganism' and the priesthood in Jerusalem centralised the sacrificial worship. Even before the Babylonian exile in the sixth century the norm was officially promulgated: one God, one people, one law, one cultus, one Temple (Deut. 12). This was the achievement of the reform of the seventh century, and behind lay the weight of the prophetic protest against sacrifice. It is best summed-up in the words of the psalmist:

I know all the fowls of the mountains: and the wild beasts of the field are mine. If I were hungry, I would not tell thee: for the world is mine, and the fullness thereof. Will I eat the flesh of bulls, or drink the blood of goats? Offer unto God the sacrifice of thanksgiving (Ps. 50:11–14).

The question of the origin of sacrifice remains. Amos asks rhetorically whether it was offered in the desert where the true Israel was fashioned. Hosea goes so far as to hold lovingkindness or mercy as the contradiction of slaughter. He and Micah seem to deny that obedience and sacrificial slaughter can be offered at the same time. Isaiah has a horror of an unrepentant and hypocritical assembly yelling their heads off in the ecstasy of blood-letting. According to the famous Psalm 51, the disposition of the penitent and his secret desire cleansed after contrition replace bloody slaughter. Man evil from conception and before birth can be transformed, not by outward gifts but by the purified will.

Yet the same Psalm 51 proclaims at the end that a purified generation may offer bulls, given the right disposition of the heart. The ambiguity remains. Nor is it confined to the gulf between the offering community and its real moral intentions on the one hand, and the objective form and substance of the offering on the other. No man can redeem his brother: this is a bold statement, but true to experience. Even given the best intentions in the world there is a limit to what I can do for you. Parents know this and have known their defeats throughout all civilisations. Curiously, a great deal can in fact be done in the business of redemption. You can redeem property, for example. Jeremiah has gone down in history as a prophet of doom who 'redeems' a plot of land outside Jerusalem when it is already in enemy hands and apparently useless. Thus his redemption stands as an acted symbol of hope. Even in terrible cases, such as kidnapping, the process of redemption works even to the present day. As long as the ransom is paid (as Angelo pretended in *Measure for Measure*) the victim may be set free. The *goel* (redeemer) in Hebrew is the next of kin who may be called upon to act by offering the ransom.

The ambiguity remains and has become even more pronounced with the passage of time. Prisoners have been ransomed in feudal times, but only if they were of good and wealthy families. Doubtful bargains have been negotiated and failed, as when the Nazis appeared to offer the lives of Jews in exchange for lorries. Since then when terrorists have taken hostages to enforce their demands for money or the release of other terrorists, it has become gradually more honourable and morally acceptable not to negotiate terms of redemption. The heroic victims are those who leave instructions for no bargains to be struck on their behalf.

In any case the payment of a ransom is the acknowledgment of a defeat. It cannot achieve any kind of reconciliation and seems outside the context of atonement. Nevertheless the instinct to buy peace and concord remains also genuine; 'the ransom of a man's life are his riches' (Prov. 13:8) and charitable causes benefit from this reasoning. It is a kind of insurance to give a ransom for every soul in the community, thus preventing disasters before they happen (Exod. 30:12 ff.). The regular payment of ransoms does not envisage kidnapping and the taking of hostages but the maintenance of good order. Thus the exchange of money, goods or properties continues when bloody sacrifices cannot be offered.

The prophetic interpretation, however, goes much further, for in the place of human payments a divine ransom alone can satisfy the need for salvation. No one puts this more eloquently than the prophet of the exile when all seemed lost and everything had to be hoped for: 'Fear not, for I have redeemed thee'. The past tense becomes the future, the miraculous and supernatural wonder when water does not drown and fire does not burn. God himself is the redeemer, the ransom are the nations, Egypt, Ethiopia and Saba. The exiled nation will be brought back in an exchange, people for people. The driving force and cause is God's love (Isa. 43:1–7). The threshold of atonement has been reached.

The Passover

'I will pass through the land of Egypt this night . . . and the blood shall be to you for a token' (Exod. 12:3 ff.). The mystery of divine action and human history converges upon the yearly feast of the *Pesach*. Every year the household is prepared for a complete change; nothing is to be left of the old, lest the evil of the past year permeate the new, as yeast causes the flour to rise. Every year the children must ask the parents 'What mean ye by this service?', for nothing about it is obvious. The orderly table with its dishes and the wine and unleavened bread, with candles lit and songs sung and tales told, is far from self-explanatory. Is a cosy family party at the heart of the ceremony? Does the merry dancing after the meal conclude a sociable togetherness? Are hosts and guests at one celebrating good neighbourliness and beginning a new year in the hope of mutual goodwill and prosperity?

Secularisation may disguise the reality and the deep chasms beneath the surface. But the asking child receives primarily a historical answer: 'It is the sacrifice of the Lord's passover, who passed over the houses of the children of Israel in Egypt, when he smote the Egyptians'. Indeed, all the stories which cluster around the Passover stress liberation against all odds, with the hasty flight from Egypt occupying the centre of the tradition. The

Lord's passover is not man's exploit but the timeless presence of God in human affairs. Thus past, present and future are rolled into one; the transcendent act unifies the fragmentation of human history. The child in asking receives the answer for the whole world, freed from the tyranny of Pharaoh. The creator God has entered history, divine power against human power.

The Passover is rooted in time and in place and it transcends time and place. It does not begin or end with the flight from Egypt. Its beginnings are shrouded in the mists of time. There are echoes of semi-nomadic shepherds who sacrifice a lamb for the flock as they migrate to a new pasture at the time of the spring equinox. Even the formal language of the institution retains the awe of the turning-point, the night when the shepherd and sheep seek protection from demonic onslaught. The apotropaic purpose is not lost as the blood of the lamb is deployed, no longer to ward off attacks on the flock but to preserve the threatened tent. The angel of destruction acknowledges the blood on the upper door posts and the lintel; while the family huddle together in safety the destroyer makes for the unprotected homes where no bunch of hyssop has sprinkled the entry.

Thus the political and military dimensions of an event which may perhaps be dated to the latter part of the thirteenth century BC are given a depth of dread. Fear and trembling pertain to the exodus, for the departing fugitives panic as soon as they have fled and the heavy chariots of the pursuers come to grief in the mud. Behind this dramatic encounter there is to be detected the contingency of human affairs. The demonic, negative, deadly character of human life, once again moving in the shadow of death, continues to hover behind the rejoicing and the triumph of the escaped slaves. The Passover despite its institutional regularity discloses the irregular, chaotic, hostile and dark which oppresses the human race and from which it is calling out for rescue. To pass over, to be passed over, because the unknown Lord passes over the terror 'not suffering the destroyer to come to smite you': this is challenge and promise.

Substitution stands at the centre of the ritual. A living thing, the lamb, must die so that the deadly danger may be averted. The rite absorbs the patriarchal drama in which Isaac was spared from the knife. Just as the boy survived and in his survival spared the father, so the Israelites survive as others die. The lamb eaten by the fellowship of the table sustains its life. It is more than a mere dish of roasted meat which may be dished up again. Nothing is to be left of it for it has become 'holy', a separate bond between all the sharers of the *Pesach* sacrifice. Its sacramental virtue ratifies not only the cohesion of the members of the covenant but also their dependence upon God.

The lamb remains the most expressive symbol of innocence. There is an unspeakable sense of sadness in the later Jewish interpretation of the helplessness of the lamb before its shearers and in the hands of its slaughterers. When Abraham, according to the ancient theme, takes the sheep from where it is caught the reader has no time to commiserate with the animal, seeing that in no other way could the promise of the future be fulfilled. But when after the Exile the righteous Servant suffers and is wounded and bruised in order to take upon himself the sins of the erring sheep and is then, like a lamb, led to the slaughter, the unbelievable silences kings and people. Here the *Aqedah* has come full circle, in as much as the original substitution, of animal for man, is enlarged to another sacrifice like a lamb, a human being, submissive, obedient unto death. Of this bloodshed we shall hear more, but it will never be understood apart from the Passover. Centuries pass, but the Passover does not pass away, for God passes over Israel and the nations in the judgment of history, in events, in new things, in personal tragedies and triumphs.

The God who 'passes over' remains transcendent and free. He comes and he goes, in human distress, heaviness, sorrow, earthquake, storm and tempest; God brings salvation by judgment upon the wilful apostates who, drunk with wine and with power, implement a covenant with death (Isa. 28:18). He comes and he goes, passing over in mercy and preserving the true foundation, the real Zion, not a refuge of lies. Thus Passover is not merely an annual feast but God in action among the peoples of the world. Every aspect of divine action may be treasured. Joshua celebrates the feast in preparation of the conquest of the land. Solomon incorporates Passover as a royal feast, celebrating kingship and stability and wealth, imploring pardon for the sins of the past. No liturgy has ever been quite as comprehensive as that given in 1 Kings 8, where the dedication of the Temple offers an opportunity to address the invisible Lord in the thick darkness of the unapproachable shrine. Here royal priesthood may be seen at work. The God beyond all worlds is 'reminded' of the covenant in supplication. Atonement derives from God's judgment: 'Hear thou in heaven and . . . forgive!', 'justify the righteous . . . condemn the wicked:'. War, drought, pestilence, plague, sickness, exile and all afflictions are in advance brought before God in prayer, for the lot of Israel and of the individual is uncertain. Even people from 'far off' are included in this solemn invocation which culminates in the great blessing. This is ratified with a holocaust of peace offerings.

No atoning ceremony is permanent in its efficacy, for no human condition abides in perfection. The disastrous development of kingship in Israel, the speedy division into two kingdoms and the decline into pagan tyranny points to the contingency and flexibility of God's passing over. Under Hezekiah of Judah, Passover is still an idyllic rite of the family as well as of the king and the priests in Jerusalem. The feast had now become enriched by regular farming, so that the agricultural season became as prominent as the pastoral calendar. Therefore the first barley harvest and thankfulness for fertile lands and good crops enter the perspective of God's beneficent presence. Wine and oil, too, bespeak God's favour. The official and the family feasting, therefore, take on a character of joyful mirth. But this could only last for a time. Even Hezekiah had intoned serious notes of penitence, and these were not to be forgotten when the kingdom of Judah tottered to its dissolution. After Josiah's death and some hopeless endeavours to save the tiny kingdom by making an alliance with Egypt, penitence rather than confident joy pertain to God's passing over. The presence of the destroyer could be felt and Jeremiah, inspired in his perception, ceases to intercede for rich and poor alike. 'Pray not for these people' is an utterance which summarises the horror of the divine visitation (Jer. 7:16; 11:14).

This Janus-like quality of the Passover confirms our experience of God in human history. Celebration answers to the good things, wailing and lamentation to the disasters. There is no neutral ground, because even divine absence is presence withdrawn. But out of this dialectic comes a third dimension, namely, the expectation that concerns the future. Ceremonies in the accepted norm continue to this day, but beyond both there is the future, the final Passover which coincides with the winding-up of the temporal order. The Messianic expectation renders the Passover universal in time and place, looking forward to the ending of time and place. The 'vacant chair' of Elijah the prophet at the Passover meal is a reminder, even in the normal setting of family and children, that all things come to an end, that a great reversal will usher in the kingdom of God.

Yom Kippur

The word *kipper* has become well-known outside the Hebrew-speaking people since the war in 1973 when the new state of Israel was nearly defeated by the Egyptians and was saved against all the odds. The Israelis were off their guard because on this day of repentance and fasting they had relaxed their military routine. The Day of Atonement thus showed to the world that it is observed by the Jewish people as a cultic obligation. It may even be reckoned to be the peak of the liturgical calendar. What is less clear is the origin of the institution and the meaning and purpose of its continuance.

A good encyclopaedia will summarise the body of the legislation, which derives mostly from Leviticus 16. The word from the root *KPR* points to the deep-seated desire of human beings to clear themselves of guilt. Before Moses and Abraham, in the cradle of the race, a loathing for pollution demanded obvious acts of cleansing. The way children even now try to conceal stains perpetuates a memory of the need to oppose dirt with purity. The first method of cleansing from a stain is to conceal the same: to 'cover up', e.g. to put an object upon the objectionable sight. Ways of removal are less likely to succeed; e.g. we soon discover that washing with water does not remove stains, but may even spread the hated evidence. The same is true of the energetic wiping away. Yet *KPR* refers to all these attempts to get back to a former condition of a clean slate.

This instinctive behaviour is ancient and preceded the cultus in Jerusalem. When the priestly class developed the rites of cleansing as an annual event it ceased to be simple and primitive. Though ablutions with water remained integral to the ceremony, the climax demanded a sacrifice in which blood was shed. Blood does not cover up, remove or wipe away, but it is shed so that God by accepting it may cover up, remove and wipe away the sins of the past, clear the community of corporate guilt and open up the way to the next year and the future. The covenant with death is voided (Isa. 28:18) because God makes reconciliation with those who offer themselves towards being reconciled in repentance. The priest mediates the sovereign act of God (Lev. 4:20). The beast carries the sins in an act of expiation, but God forgives and cleanses from all sins which pollute the land and defile the congregation.

But the rite is wonderfully mysterious because no simple slaughter is involved when the priest, dressed in linen vestments, takes two goats as a sin-offering and a ram as a burnt-offering for the community, and a bullock as a sin-offering for himself. Lots are cast for the two goats: one for the Lord, one for Azazel. The blood of one victim cleanses the sanctuary. The body of the other becomes the sin-carrier, for the priest lays his hands on it and confesses the sins of Israel over it. The scapegoat is then expelled into the desert, probably taken by another priest and thrown over a precipice.

We have no eye-witnesses of the procedure and know nothing of the psychological and spiritual impact of the annual rite on the people. Standing in the area of the Temple in Jerusalem imagination fails one in the reconstruction of what happened and where. There have even been suggestions that the written documents are no more than literary fragments and not descriptions of events that took place. On the other hand, anthropologists such as Frazer collected evidence from all over the globe to prove the universality of the scapegoat as a sacrificial offering. It certainly symbolises something, possibly a sexual urge or lust, as associated with the god Pan and the satyrs. Moreover the notion that guilt can be passed on, through a trick played by children with their 'it was him or her' charge, or even an imaginative double playing the part of the other, has become again an outstanding feature in criminal cases. The criminal, like the child which has offended, seeks a scapegoat, and quite often the lies that have been told to invent the 'other' succeed only too well. The 'I did not do it, some other person or persons did it' becomes a valid form of defence which has to be disproved by the prosecution. This line of defence was attempted at the trial of war criminals and still invites debate many years after Nuremberg. The question in law and in ethics is quite simply one of liability and responsibility. If the higher or lower rank of officer of an extermination squad can prove that he killed under orders which he could not evade he may be acquitted. In this unexpected way the scapegoat has returned from the mists of anthropology and mythology to a world terrorised by evil.

But the scapegoat itself is not devilish; it carries the intolerable burden of sins, but it has not sinned. Therefore the demonic and arcane nature of the rite lies not with the goat but with the recipient of the goat. Now this Azazel remains a totally unexplained and inexplicable part of the narrative. One can only speculate that the name had once some meaning that is now lost. It is certainly associated with the lifeless desert, the dreaded world of snakes, scorpions and hyenas. Be that as it may, once the demonic realm is mentioned as a possible designation, all kinds of dualism creep into the Day of Atonement. Let the sin return to where it comes from! There is an evil power, hidden from men and women but always active and powerful, which once a year has to be appeased and whose assaults have to be warded off, not by blood, but by the sacrifice of a whole living animal. Like unto like, the terrified beast, as a substitute, is given to the source of the terror. As we shall see, this dualistic view of human existence and sin can never quite disappear from our understanding of terror among us. Once this enemy in the desert is identified with the Satan of the book of Job or equivalents like Beelzebub and Lucifer and furthermore with the unspeakable murderers of our time, we enter a sphere in which even the annual corporate guilt seems a mere triviality. A modern scapegoat seems also unimaginable, for what sort of being could innocently carry away like some nuclear waste the horrors of the past? The truth is that the whole world seeks for such scapegoats and cannot find them. They are extinct.

In Jewish liturgical developments the demonic has been exorcised. This can be no great wonder, for without the Temple and the priesthood (after AD 70) the whole ritual could only survive as a recital. However much we may talk about re-enactment upon stage and in recitals, nothing can take the place of sacrifice itself. A real scapegoat is very different from mere talk about it; realism and symbolism do not always meet. But quite apart from the palpable impossibility of restoring sacrifice among the dispersed Jews, the whole tendency of law and commentary was anti-demonic and anti-mysterious. The Yom Kippur is deprived of sacrifice, and fasting takes the place of animals and their life-blood. The prayers do not require a priest but a singer who chants, with the congregation, towards the presence: 'Our God and God of our fathers, pardon our iniquities on this Day of Atonement; blot out our transgressions and our sins and make them pass away from before thine eyes.' The Jewish prayer book is very specific in self-accusations: God and God alone blots out the sins of the arrogant and stiff-necked people, who have been faithless, have robbed, done violence, have forged lies, have scoffed, have blasphemed; in short, have gone astray. A distinction is made between sins freely committed and those committed under compulsion. Everything is laid open before the all-seer and total remission is entreated. No absolution is given except the recall of God as the God of Israel, who answers the perplexing question of guilt and the helplessness of man. When the *shofar* is sounded the congregation can dismiss itself and break the fast at home. But has atonement been achieved? This search confronts not only Jews but also the whole world with renewed pain and intensity.

'Christ died for us'

The fragmentation of our world rules out a simple solution to conflict. Heraclitus of Ephesus, c.500 BC, chides the illusion of peace: 'Homer was wrong in saying "Would that strife might perish from gods and men". He did not see that he was praying for the destruction of the universe' (*Fragments*, 43,44). Heraclitus might well be pleased with our immersion in endless and insoluble strife. But destruction is now more likely to come from war than from peace. We are restless and warlike to the end.

From a practical point of view we experience this war on more levels than did the ancient world. Then the affront to the gods and the profanation of the mysteries caused a miasma and the need for cleansing the pollution of putrescent matter was obvious. Similarly political and military disasters proved that wanton violence and outrages of all kinds are repaid in a chain of cause and effect. The wise and the uncorrupt could refute the blindness of infatuated fools and point to the fruits of reckless tyrannies. All these poisons and pests, physical and metaphysical, could be contained by restraints of law or by religious purifications. Angry powers could be propitiated; failing that revenge and collapse squared the account. Private lives and private quarrels, too, came within the orbit of the inevitable. Intentions, deeds and guilt could be identified. The great tragedies personalise the stakes of life and death, so that Oedipus, Ajax, Iphigenia, Antigone and Philoctetes become the symbols of the tragic sense of life.

Our experience lies on different planes. The world is not peopled with heroes any more. There is indeed a lot of unmysterious pollution on land and in the sea, some of it caused by acid rain. There are industrial wastelands, dying forests, poisoned lakes and contaminated rivers. But the causes and the effects differ from the sequences in the ancient world. We are governed by economic considerations and technological advances, a new determinism without religious significance. Airports and casinos, factories and entertainments, communications and propaganda are powers in themselves, financed and run by states or agencies of states or privately. The whole sociological framework which derives from the politico-economic bloc lies outside the points of reference of the religious vocabulary. There is no tragedy and no tragic symbol to enshrine our experience of these things.

It may be different with voluntary organisations and private lives. But the weight of neutral events and institutions seems to undo centuries of spirituality. Churches and sects may seek reconciliation but soon form committees which discuss peace formulae in the accepted fashion of parliaments or congresses. This is not surprising, for personal language and feeling can only come face to face and mouth to mouth, not committee to committee. Even families flee from the direct and often tragic manner of reconciliation. They do not know, or they dislike to speak or listen in, terms of expiation, propitiation, redemption, restitution, sacrifice and atonement. It is against this background of alienation that Christian claims must be restated.

These Christian claims, however, are as fragmented as the world itself. As already stressed, no Council of the Church ever produced a monolithic definition of atonement or of the work of Christ. But even if they did not understand the liturgical formulations, the worshippers knew where they stood or ought to stand. Catholics affirmed the sacrifice and in endless ways reiterated the perpetuation of this sacrifice in the mass: *'Suscipe, sancte Pater, omnipotens aeterne Deus, hanc immaculatam hostiam'* or *'Veni, sanctificator omnipotens aeterne Deus et benedic hoc sacrificium'*. The priest and the congregation pray for their sacrifice to be accepted and so on until the end of mass. The reformers protested against this repetition of the sacrifice. They stressed the once-and-for-allness of the sacrifice on the cross. The Anglican version of the Book of Common Prayer summarises all that has been achieved by Christ's death in the following formulation: 'for our redemption; who made there (by his one oblation of himself once offered) a full, perfect, and sufficient sacrifice, oblation and satisfaction, for the sins of the whole world'. This is perpetually remembered as a holy institution in remembrance of the death and passion of Jesus. The intending communicants are in fact taken back to the solemn night when Jesus gave himself as body and blood.

This unified view of sacrifice which telescopes and implies a great many of atonement rites, ideas and traditions, is now replaced by a multiform liturgical language. The pluralism of cultures and religions has invaded the Christian tradition itself. The broadest spectrum of views may permit a toleration of contradictory beliefs about Jesus, the death of Jesus, the remembering of the Last Supper and of his Atonement.

The only agreed starting point is the universal conviction that the death of Jesus has something to do with our conflicts and sufferings and longing for better things. This is not very much and certainly not enough to inspire anyone. Even this admission opens up doors to controversial views, for the death of Jesus, more than that of Socrates or any other famous figure, remains the centre of disputed claims. 'Why was Jesus killed?' is the simple question which receives almost as many answers as there are professors of the New Testament. But even apart from this specific problem there lies behind it the far more acute uncertainty of how to place Jesus in his time. Before we can account for the indictment which led to his death we have to know something about this son of man, Son of

God, son of Mary and Joseph, the Christ. He has not left any memoirs or other documentation. Therefore, we have to be content to read the few documents that can be dated to within decades of his lifetime, mostly in the New Testament and a few outside, to form an opinion of this Jew among Jews, this preacher among Pharisees, this sectarian among others, this pacifist among revolutionaries, this man from Galilee in Jerusalem, this lone rabbi among his disciples. All the titles bestowed upon him may throw some light upon his parentage, his home, his craft, his successes and his failures. Even then we can hardly say much about him. We do not know what he looked like, what languages he spoke, whether Greek, Hebrew, Aramaic, perhaps even a little Latin, what education he had apart from carpentry, whether he could or could not write. Of his inner life we know even less and of the length of his ministry, from the call of the disciples to the end, we are ignorant. He was crucified in Jerusalem, on some Friday, possibly in what is now called AD 29.

Yet this shameful death, this 'hanging on the tree', brings together all the disparate appraisals of Jesus. That such an execution, such a horrible degradation of the human body, should symbolise a cosmic redemption which encompasses every existing conflict is the miracle which Christians ascribe to God the creator, the redeemer and the Holy Spirit. All the elements of conflict and atonement are locked together in the gospels. Neutral or normal conditions seem to be ruled out. There is a crisis in human affairs, an either – or challenge. If it is not accepted, only division and perdition can prevail. Hence behind all the earthly powers there is a dark and Satanic hostile army which invades religious institutions, governmental privileges, families and followers. Jesus is seen during his short ministry to fight with temptations and to engage in an inner struggle to overcome this power. Before his death he does not atone but he heals wherever possible. He both condemns and denounces in the prophetic manner and he forgives. The whole paradox of love and rejection is felt by him as well as being actively heightened by his words and deeds. Jesus is both master

CHRIST DIED FOR US

and servant, giving and receiving, withdrawing from and entering into the world, fleeing from contact with crowds and working among them, powerful and powerless, rich and poor. If Kierkegaard commented on Abraham that he 'could not understand him', our reaction to the Jesus of the gospels is summarised by St Paul, who said that we do not know him any longer 'after the flesh'. Yet in a sense Christians would also affirm that they know Jesus better than they know themselves or their nearest relations and friends. This paradox is inseparable from the work of Christ.

The climax of the paradox is reached in the agony, the arrest, the trial and the execution of Jesus. The ordeal of a tragic hero can be grasped, but not the submission of the creator to his creatures. True, pagan gods, such as Heracles, Aphrodite and Persephone, were presented as sufferers, mostly in accordance with the seasons and the woes of the natural world. But the suffering of Jesus has nothing of the pagan charm. All the figures and prophesies of the past seem to converge upon the final act in the Garden of Gethsemane, the praetorium in Jerusalem and the hill of the skull. The narratives lack any didactic insistence that this death is atonement in itself. Jesus, however, had at the Last Supper identified his forthcoming death with the Passover sacrifice and the giving of himself with a payment, a ransom. The promise of the Messiah who comes as a servant pertained to the secret now to be revealed in the actuality of self-giving. But, above all, Jesus was the beloved son of the father, the Isaac of Genesis 22, who had to be bound by his father in fulfilment of the unacceptable order. Thus Jesus enters into the total darkness of abandonment, the eclipse of all hope and the state of dereliction now known to the post-Holocaust generation. The Kafkaesque fantasy and the death camp reality and grip of totalitarian power evoke the universal echo to the single verse: 'My God, my God, why hast thou forsaken me?'. No longer dare anyone interpret these words as a quotation from Psalm 22 cited by Jesus on the cross as a kind of gloss; rather the words articulate the despair of the victim of physical, mental and spiritual torture.

The mystery of Good Friday and Holy Saturday has never ceased to move generations, churches, individuals and mystics of all races. The unrelieved suffering, the agony and the death, followed by the descent from the cross and the burial, have been depicted, contemplated and transposed into music. Most strangely this scene of horror has opened a vision of light, and despair has yielded to hope. The liturgies from Palm Sunday until the beginning of Easter surround the inexplicable mystery of defeat, defamation and annihilation of one in a remote corner of time and space.

But for centuries, alas, the mystery has failed to atone, for it has divided Jews and Christians. The murder of God, deicide, has until 1965 been ascribed to the 'perfidious' Jews. The response to the solemn question: 'O my people, what have I done to thee?' has been pogroms in eastern Europe. The *crux fidelis*, the *dulce lignum* (sweet cross, sweet wood) became terrifying symbols and failed to speak of the benefits of the cross. Instead of acclaiming the God of the exodus as the self-giving liberator, the crowds enthroned Satan to consummate hatred in genocide. Thus the crucified and the gassed became one.

This oneness still remains to be grasped by Jews and Christians and the world. Great things are indeed afoot, and the words from the cross penetrate the darkness as never before. 'Father, forgive them, for they know not what they do' are not words to condone irresponsibility but to challenge the indifferent. The threadbare stock excuse 'we did not know', uttered by people who could smell the decomposition in the camps (e.g. Buchenwald), meets with indignation. Repentance for atrocities and for crimes can be sincere and is traditionally associated with the contemplation of the cross. Christ, surrounded by two thieves, as narrated in Luke's gospel, attracts defiance as well as penitence. Forgiveness takes the form of a dramatic promise: 'Today thou shalt be with me in paradise'. No acquittal or promise is extended to the guilty who remain unrepentant. The Passion appeals to the freedom of repentance.

How succeeding generations and individuals have responded to the crucifixion is a matter of history. Understandably they have endeavoured to distance themselves from the physical grossness of the degradation of the human body. They have veiled the stark reality. Thus crucifixes of all shapes and of high and low quality have reconciled the owners and the beholders to their fate and even to death. Identification in death not only helped and comforted the suffering but also promoted ascetic mortifications, dying to sin by killing the impulses and instincts.

In the light of our experiences much has remained of this fellowship in suffering. For example, the testimonies which come from communist countries show how people with a Christ-centred faith endure appalling torments in labour camps and 'hospitals'. Their faith enables them not only to bear the pain and the nervous tension but also the wickedness of the authorising tormentors. The crucifiers are the liars, and the crucified cherish the truth with the Christ in their midst. A biography, such as Solzhenitsyn's or Mandelstamm's, tells us more about martyrdom and the freedom of truth in martyrdom than any medical treatise or sociological report. *Ecce homo*! *Ecce* men and women! So also in the German concentration camps where the Hitler demons killed in order to kill the God of the Jews and where the martyrs wept, prayed and aided one another. Above all, seeing the crucifixion through our experience we are reconciled to death. The old enemy has become our friend.

Yet much remains unanswered, and experience is a shaky asset by itself. Even the New Testament writers stand back and distance themselves from the ugly sight and the smell of corruption in order to interpret this death. The Fourth Gospel pioneers the paradox that the man on the gallows is the king of the universe. The *Logos* which was before the world was created, the eternal truth, strides in royal procession to his throne of glory. The hour of glory coincides with the execution, for it is then that the Son hands himself to the Father in complete obedience. In a metaphysical web of relationships the triumph of God's love is set forth. Even in the agony of dying the king rules, unites mother and disciple and thus the whole mystical fellowship of the king's subjects. The King of the Jews becomes through his obedience the king of the redeemed, offering himself in death to the Father and to them by the Holy Spirit. This act is intellectually beyond human comprehension; how can the abstract reality – Logos – truth, which is precosmic, rule and suffer in the flesh of Jesus, son of Mary?

The Johannine paradox of triumph is set against the mysterious canvas of the Passover. Not only is Jesus the lamb recalling Genesis 22 and Isaiah 53 and the celebrant of the feast, but Jesus as the Son objectifies and eternalises his death as the sacrifice of cosmic proportions. The evangelist does not see degradation and corpses, but exodus and freedom; not necessity and destruction, but love between Father and Son sent forth and returning. One might say that the ordeal of Abraham and Isaac is transcended by a cosmic reconciliation.

Triumph through death is not our experience, even if we can allow for release from suffering through death. But the Pauline view and interpretation of this execution, as Paul may or may not have seen, is precisely this. The triumph of victory pertains to the humble and anonymous servant, because of what he is in himself and what he does for his loved ones. Indeed, for Paul there is no conquest of evil and no progess towards divine citizenship except by identification with the Christ in suffering. He also takes over the older view that the prisoners and debtors are 'bought' and set free by the ransom (1 Cor. 6:20; 7:23). Similarly 1 Peter repeats the theme that neither gold nor silver but precious blood has redeemed the corrupt and thereby fulfilled the purpose of creation (1:18 ff.).

The paradox of life-giving and life-obtaining is even more systematically and rhetorically set forth in the Epistle to the Hebrews. Christ is here priest and victim, of the celestial sanctuary and of the place of execution on earth. The writer reaches the peak of his exposition in chapter 9 where the sacred cultus provides the canvas to an eternal and metaphysical reality of sacrifice. As Philo and others before him, he sees the atonement rite as a shadow or type of reality. For him the key is to be found in the 'how much more' of the fulfilment of intimations and anticipations. He stresses the 'once and for all' of the death of Christ, but he clearly interprets all martyrdoms as microcosmic copies of the macrocosmic perfection. Everything moves towards crisis, towards acceptance or condemnation, and atonement is the key of our destiny.

We have reached a turning-point. From now on no human or animal sacrifice is needed or even permitted. The unique sacrifice of the Christ outside Jerusalem continues at the heavenly altar beyond space and time. Thus atonement in all its forms and aspects falls within the structure which we call hierarchical. The high priest stands at the apex of being and offers himself to God in mutual acceptance. Everything that can be seen, heard and touched is a reflection of this sacrificial unity. Whatever we experience or represent as human beings in the immensity of the universe corresponds to the transcendent, if our experience displays any merit, or suffering, witnessing to the truth, generosity of character or striving after perfection.

Looking into this mirror of uncreated light and energy we have no difficulty in concluding that the unspeakable evil, which always throws shadows of disgust, will be burnt up and end in the very ashes of non-being which it administered to the innocent and the righteous. In a flash and with much weeping I realised this when I stood in Berlin-Plötzensee[1] at the execution block. In this prison men and women of all classes and with or without belief were hanged without mercy. Their names and their deeds reflect the light and their sufferings corresponded to the priestly act of the lamb. The butchers reflect nothing and correspond to nothing. Thus atonement unites and divides.

This paradox confronts us with ferocity in our age of brutality. Not only at Plötzensee Prison but at all the shrines where the dead are commemorated as martyrs for the truth we feel the proximity of the death of Jesus as well as the distance. The latter is not only due to the identity of the martyrs who were often not baptized, professed no faith in God, followed a political conviction or simply did their duty as their conscience bade them.

Their distance from the sacrificial claims and the communion of saints excludes them from the key figures mentioned in the Tridentine mass: *'munera pueri tui justi Abel, et sacrificium Patriarchae nostri Abrahae: et quod tibi obtulit summus sacerdos tuus Melchisedech'*.They had probably never heard of the gifts of just Abel, the *Aqedah* or the binding of Isaac, the sacrifice of Abraham or the mysterious priesthood of Melchizedek. But this distance does not prevent us from joining them. Anne Frank, Edith Stein, Father Kolbe and Dietrich Bonhoeffer, along with innumerable men and women, named and unnamed, are offered by the eternal high priest to the Father.

The dogmatic claim is not softened by this inclusion. If the death of Christ is the universal sacrifice for sin which 'takes away' the sin, then expiation and reconciliation have an objective and infinite value. The witness in our history brings near what was distant, for sacrifice has become fact. All the theories ring true up to a point but they are always transcended by reality. The 'ransom is paid' in and by faithful humanity in self-oblation. The free act of voluntary, or even enforced, dying has 'paid a debt', for our martyrs did what we could not do and took our place. But their heroism could not satisfy the tragic desolation of our existence unless it were lifted to the one perfect act in which manhood is accepted in the Godhead. The distance no longer separates, for we experience as fact that 'neither death, nor life . . . nor things present, nor things to come . . . shall be able to separate us from the love of God, which is in Christ Jesus our Lord'. The greater the distance in death the more abundant the gracious acceptance of sacrifice. This is the vision in Plötzensee and everywhere.

. . . And rise again on the third day

Atonement among human beings is as paradoxical, fragmentary and unfinished as they themselves. Time and again one meets people who seem to have reached perfection, serenity and peace. But this peace is deceptive. Our margins of tolerance are thin. Take away this comfort, that inhibition, and, above all, trust and faith in others, and the skeleton appears without the flesh of good intentions and regular habits. Atonement does not spell human triumph. This triumph lies in the future, yet to be attained. Even St Paul has no doubt that he himself must still achieve his celestial destiny, or rather that it must be achieved for him, for everything is of grace, given freely and undeservedly. Hence all the prayers of the faithful take into account the needy and end with an incantation that all may be well at the end and beyond the end. Death of the individual is still the full stop, and death of communities and civilisations frightens the world.

Only the Christ has entered into his glory after death, and his resurrection occurred on earth as the starting point of the new world. The Ascension and the departure of the living Christ is not counted as a disaster but as the completion of the atoning sacrifice. The Resurrection ratifies the acceptance of the victim as the priest who mediates humanity to the Godhead. This reconciliation is final and not subject to fragmentation and alteration. Three gospels (not Mark's) report the reversal of all earthly experience as if it were something that ought to have been known. It was prophesied, predicted and has happened.

It was the resurrection that created the Christian Church; scriptures, liturgies, missions, ministries, martyrdoms and even struggles and splits are unthinkable apart from faith in him who rose on the third day. But it is also a faith which abolishes time and duration, for that which lies in the past is present in the now and opens the future. The resurrection of the dead is inseparable from atonement for, as Irenaeus states in a celebrated passage: 'He became what we are, that he might make us what he is.' Hence the divinisation of man is another term for the new life, and the resurrection is not only the authentic seal of our immortal destiny, but also of the universal and eternal future, in which from now on physical death is but an incident. True, many writers still tend to interpret death as an enemy force, almost as a punishment to be endured. In as much as Christian realists are forced to acknowledge that evil is still in our midst, seduces and often rules, the Satanic régime makes its demands, and death is a kind of payment to Satan. But this payment is redeemed by God in the resurrection of the faithful and the righteous.

Indeed, an optimistic appraisal of the human condition does not prevail in the history of Christian thought. The giants, such as Augustine, were pessimistic enough and they were proved right in their estimation. 'The world is very evil', resurrection or no resurrection. Only a total otherworldliness, as lived and developed by some mystics, can step outside the norms of conflict and celebrate absolute reconciliation through nonparticipation.

To the outsider, coming afresh to the material of past centuries, it must come as a surprise that it voices often, if not mostly, a deep-seated pessimism. Its beginning may be found in the New Testament itself, probably when persecution was pressing upon the members of the community. Though Jesus is hailed as the faithful martyr and the firstborn of the dead (Rev. 1:5) and the Christians are incessantly encouraged to rejoice, darker tones are also heard. After all, to put to silence the ignorance of brutal fools and to endure patiently under wrongful arrest and accusation do not come naturally, however strong the exhortation to the imitation of Christ (1 Pet. 2). A 'spiritual sacrifice' (Heb. 13:15) in a covenant relationship with God is theoretically very fine and often cited in liturgies. But to carry undeserved punishment is more likely to lead to deep resentment. And once hatred meets hatred the old curse lies upon the righteous too; the Acts of the Apostles openly depicts hostile relationships. It has often been observed that men can deal heroically with apocalyptic antagonists and lose the spiritual battle *en famille*, i.e. in the trivialities of the passing scene. Church history, like all history, is a record of the inefficacy of New Testament exhortation and ethics. Hence the waning of the apostolic optimism of the kind articulated in Paul's letter to the Colossians, where the death and the resurrection of Christ have made peace. The Ephesians were admonished to celebrate a new structure of universal harmony which replaces the old outworn rubbish. No doubt Paul went to his death in this unshaken and unshakeable hope of cosmic reconciliation. Even if Christian converts would go to the pagan courts, as in Corinth, Paul would remind them of the high price paid for their redemption and win his case.

A bifocal vision enforces a dualistic reaction to things as they are. On the one hand, Christ is risen and with him the creation is lifted to God in cosmic harmony; on the other the devil strides upon the earth, seeking whom he may devour, and reigning for a short time. The liturgies proclaim peace, 'my peace', and the risen presence in the sacred meal; and the world outside the catacombs, in later years outside basilicas and churches, and in later centuries still within churches, rages in cruelties and destruction. The apocalyptic strains in the New Testament openly declare that there is war, not only on earth but also in heaven. Christ risen and ascended reigns in the kingdom of his Father and through the spirit in the Church, but Satan too reigns in every conceivable evil.

The great classical theologians wrestle unsuccessfully with the insoluble. Logical explanations are pushed aside by fanciful pictures which show a devil baited and himself deceived, the theme of the cheater cheated, which not only attracted giants like Augustine, Gregory, Peter Lombard and Bernard of Cluny, but also Goethe's disciples in our own time. Of all these men of genius, Augustine stands out as the one who explores the irrational with rational logic. His knowledge of the risen Christ and of the triumph of transcendent truth clashes with his encounters with the lie and not with a mythological monster called the devil. Having been himself trapped by the city of this earth, he must reconcile its continuance with the risen Christ in his soul.

Augustine's genius spans the two worlds of the risen Christ and the demonic world, especially in his best-known works, the *Confessions* and *The City of God*. The impact of them has been immense. From the start they delineate the personal life, from beginning to mid-point, from pagan exuberance to philosophical despair and thence to Christian conversion, on the one hand; on the other there is the chaos of the ever-shifting corporate world, always influencing us, tearing us to pieces and surviving us with its impersonal strength. To seek atonement in such a divided world defies intellectual analysis, but, as Augustine would observe, to say nothing would amount to defeat.

Confessions is about people who looked beyond martyrdom into themselves. Augustine does not shrink from revealing himself, a boy who stole pears and an ambiguous lover of a mistress. Passions and disgust run through his life with a yearning for the real life. By the time of writing his autobiography around AD 397, he was a bishop and cut off from Italy and sophisticated debate. He could see in retrospect his own life so far as a symbol of the redeeming work of the exalted Christ. Thus classical rhetoric, Platonic idealism and scriptural claims could articulate the strange work of a God who buys the prisoners from the closed prison. Sin stood between him and his past, and death separated him from mother and friends. We learn one thing immediately: this fissure in human existence can only be rendered in human speech if the speech is directed to God. One cannot talk about it; one can only talk to him.

Augustine has become the classical exponent of Christian belief as he reviews himself, his miseries and failures. God's act of Atonement is always present as he addresses 'God, my sweetness', 'O my late joy', the creator, redeemer and the spirit. Extremely abstract truths mingle with down-to-earth reminiscences. It is not the outer world that matters; the inner world, namely, the soul, is real. The 'bleeding soul' which flounders in the void suffers from the wrong sense of delight. The soul is attracted to vandalism, which is the very paradigm of freewill abused. Augustine, accordingly, does not hold that the atoning work of Christ settles upon human nature, but rather that from birth a corrupt will dictates a compulsive urge to commit evil. There is nothing good about a child who engages in habits which will form a chain. For Augustine even the child at the mother's breast does not yield an idyllic picture but rather a manifestation of human nature in 'sucking dry'. Not sins but sin comes into focus as a prenatal disposition. Yet this sinful creature is meant for eternity and cannot circumvent its destiny. There is a deep memory in us which may yearn for the truth. It stirred in Augustine himself in the great crisis which led to his conversion. But conversion does not end with dramatic happenings, nor does confession terminate sinfulness. The love which responds to the love of God is a healing love which must grow.

Augustine's pessimism disowns self-reliance and human help. Man is bound with bonds which he cannot break; grace liberates the prisoner. The mutuality of God's free act and the human response is nothing new but central to the biblical tradition. Psalm 27: 8 expresses this strange work of God in unforgettable brevity: 'Seek ye my face; my heart said unto thee, Thy face, Lord, will I seek.' For Augustine this is the key to the secret door: to seek the face of God is to be sought by God[1]. In this sense it is also true that 'to him who has, it shall be given' (Matt. 13:12). The seeking of the face of God is not an effort of the human will but divine grace.

The seeking God abides with his risen presence in the midst of our miseries. The Christian is on the road to

Emmaus and enters the inn with the stranger (Luke. 24:13). Emmaus comes to symbolise the happy moment when disciples, free from envy and self-seeking, say to the unknown presence 'stay with us!'. Augustine and all Christian theologians universalise this personal encounter. Emmaus is the ideal state which church membership and sacramental sharing in the Eucharist set before Christians as the goal. Emmaus also comes to symbolise the blindness of the world where others at the inn do not know or care to know what is happening. Rembrandt's famous picture portrays the servant at the table in complete ignorance of the event.

Despite his pessimism, Augustine confirms the tradition which guides human life from baptism to burial in the constant process of a learning discipline. The soul is constantly being weaned from perversion; it is being reconciled to God by God and not by man. If it endures more suffering on the way this may be accepted as punishment or as a goad. On the highest level, suffering may even expiate the sins of others as Christ suffered for the unrighteous.

If atonement were restricted to personal salvation by punishment, repentance and acceptance, our problems would still be daunting but not insurmountable. But the social and political power, and its penetration of the soul, adds a dimension which every Christian would wish away. St Paul had already weighed up the pros and cons of this – and other – worldliness: 'I am in a strait betwixt the two, having the desire to depart and be with Christ; for it is very far better; yet to abide in the flesh is more needful for your sake' (Phil. 1:21 ff.). Augustine, too, would have been a happier man detached from this world. He knew this well enough. In the heavenly Jerusalem there is peace, and the contemplative, at peace with himself, can lose himself in true citizenship. In and about AD 410, when Rome was sacked by the Goths, who would not want to run away? How much worse in 1933 when Hitler came to power and in 1940 when escape had become impossible! Many Christian voices repeat the desire to quit. In 1950 Julien Green notes in his diary that the desire to quit is sometimes so strong that he does not know how to resist. It is a great temptation, but God's act of Atonement counters the desire to give in, though the soul can do no more than weep and offer a broken heart.

Augustine leads the way of resistance in the confusion. Despite chaos and disasters he addresses 'citizens of Jerusalem' as God's people, who do not belong here but elsewhere. There are two cities, inextricably mixed, Babylon and Jerusalem. Merely to denounce the former and to foretell judgment is not enough. Nor is our religious instinct to keep what we have got a sure guide. Augustine has no patience with his enemies who blame Christians for the disasters because they abandoned the old religion of Rome. The Christian with a claim to universal salvation cannot abominate change in the world. He must embrace the future while being aware of the demonic nature of all tyrannies and lies. He can absorb the evil by making history before God. This attitude to world events may be called 'prophetic' history and it sets the whole complex of atonement in a universal setting. It is no wonder that Augustine's *The City of God* became, despite all its confusion, a light during the Dark Ages. It enabled Europe to rise again after endless defeats and catastrophes. And still, to speak with Augustine, we serenade the heavenly Jerusalem and, with Christ, weep over the earthly Jerusalem.

Augustine's radical estimate of human nature and society became a lasting strength, for the delusions of the earthly city need to be spelt out unless atonement is to become a useless sentimentality. The structure and energy of the earthly city derive from rivalry, envy and hatred. The Cainish destroyers never cease to operate and they can be identified in every century and in every land. Yet there are the chosen pilgrims, not only individuals but also communities, who strive after harmony. In this bizarre life of horrors and gratuitous sufferings there is the foundation of potential goodness, which reflects health in sickness, charity in war, light in darkness. The cosmic perspective comes to our aid in discerning the omnipotent lordship in the true city of God for which the Christ suffered and in which he rose from the dead.

Cum Sancto Spiritu . . .

Augustine had the good fortune to die before the arrival of the Vandals and the total destruction of his see. Even he would have been amazed to witness the ensuing catastrophe which culminated in the loss of Africa to Islam. Losses abounded on all sides and for centuries only darkness ruled. The City of the earth was in charge. The chronicle of disasters is so unbroken and all-embracing that the talk of atonement, reconciliation and recapitulation seems hollow and meaningless. Christian churches, institutions and corporate bodies vied with each other in strife. Wherever possible Christians fought for supremacy with unsurpassed cruelty. After the split of the Reformation whole countries were laid waste in war and through famine. Hatred of the Jews was encouraged, pogroms raged. But the mechanisation of evil in every form is the post-Christian climax of a demonic society, and Hitler's concentration camps and extermination of millions, the Gulag Archipelago and the Asian and African horrors no longer answer to any norms of religion, rationality and human feeling. The litany of monstrous, meaningless and agonising places, criminals and harvests of evil is too long to be rendered. Only a never-ending cry of despair and protest pervades the universe: City of earth, may you perish, may you vanish out of sight, hearing and memory!

May your lies be exposed! May you, devils and monsters behind the lies, be judged, condemned, sentenced and consumed in the hatred you have sown and garnered!

Whether in a formal litany or a legal indictment, a lamentation, a lone voice, innocent blood finds its means of utterance, of accusation. It cannot tolerate false interpretation of guilt and atonement. One lesson, one poem, one account read from the endless pages of notes taken from survivors, witnesses against the blasphemous notion that forgiveness through human effort is possible. Anselm and Calvin had the right instinct when they saw atonement in this severe light. Man, they insisted, cannot expiate; only God can wipe out the foul pollution, made so much worse since Augustine, Anselm and Calvin prayed and reflected.

How then can the divine justice be tempered with mercy? If retributive justice is of the essence of divine government, does all corruption lead to a hell of endless punishment? The very devilishness of the tormentors of our age enforces a far greater sensitivity to the measuring of sin, and thus to the quality of both justice and mercy. To start with, the common guilt of man is not to be identified for a moment with the outrages and their perpetrators. The common and inherited sin of Adam is 'covered' by the death of the second Adam: 'For as in Adam all die, so in Christ all shall be made alive'. There is no self-worship, no 'Pelagian' justification by works, in declaring that the benefits of Christ's death and resurrection are made available to the helpless victims of violence. There could be no condemnation of these partakers of his cross, who are, not by choice but by destiny, 'in Christ Jesus'. The law of the Spirit of life in Christ Jesus continues God's gracious acceptance of souls. If this be called universalism it clearly does not condone perverse criminality.

Through the Spirit all things are changed and redeemed. Bodies have been killed, souls tortured, faces spat upon. All is made good after death and an all-embracing mercy extends to the living souls, not for their righteous works, which they were prevented from working, but through the work of the Spirit. Atonement without the spiritual resurrection is impossible. God works in Christ Jesus through the Holy Spirit and imparts eternal light to the people in deep darkness. Thus from east to west is a people reborn by the Spirit. Christ as the priest offers through the Spirit the slaughtered and murdered. Justice is restored in the universe by the Spirit.

How then are the innocent raised from nothing? If there is nothing, no seed can be buried (John 12:24), no new house can be found to be dwelt in (2 Cor. 5). The slaughter of bodies is brought to the finest art by the falsehood of Marxist-Leninist denials of the human soul. Even Augustine and Aquinas did not have to battle against this predominant blasphemy, which has reached such proportions of strength that even Christians and Jews have openly or tacitly yielded to the materialistic anthropology. Hitler and his henchmen never bothered themselves about souls, just as individual murderers and rapists do not give a thought to the immortal souls of their victims. How is it possible for Christians, among them theologians, to go against the fundamental 'Christ has been raised from the dead . . . It is sown a natural body; it is raised a spiritual body' (1 Cor. 15)? We have reached an impasse unknown to our forefathers.

Dialectical materialism, itself the child of socialist propositions before Marx as well as of Darwinian evolutionism, has crept into theology and thence into practical and practised Christianity. This materialistic anthropology dismisses the existence of the soul and with its special vocabulary from sociology puts into its place a collective humanity, a species of advanced anthropoid. To make matters worse and more convincing, such propositions of soulless man are alleged to be true to Hebrew psychology. A case is made out for the living soul *nephesh* not to be the *anima*, the breath which gives life to dust and clay, but to be merely a word for something like 'self'. Thus modern translations of the Bible without warning the hapless client, hardly ever translate *Nephesh* as 'soul'. This convenient form of forgery, which incidentally has also affected the translation of Freud into English (as Bruno

Bettelheim has proved in *Freud and Man's Soul*), has also invaded texts translated from the New Testament. Once granted that the individual human soul does not exist, it is one further step to denounce individualism, to belittle the importance of persons as such, and even to regard sins and sinfulness as trivial. The only sin, said a poster in a French Catholic church a few years ago, is individualism. Churches with their ambition to be on good terms with the world and to secure a place in religious competitiveness have always been tempted to replace the eternal I with an ongoing we, and this is precisely what has been done in some churches in the recital of the creed. *'Credo'* with its affirmation of the soul as authentic and indestructible has been replaced by 'we believe'. Thus the damnation of the wicked and the resurrection of the righteous are neutralised by collectivism, by the faceless 'we'.

The immortality of the soul, and therefore of all souls, is indispensable to any hope and therefore to a yearning for atonement. The bodies of all animals, as of all humans, are known to decompose and they can never be united eternally to God. It is only the spirit in man, which resides in the soul, which strives to be made one with the spirit of God. The denial of this immortality not only undoes our humanity but also the resurrection of Christ; as St Paul clearly stated in his great peroration of 1 Corinthians 15, if there is no resurrection of the dead all our hopes are vain.

We move here beyond a psychological estimate or an anthropological insight. Rather, looking at the ocean of innocent lives, arrested, trapped, outraged and killed, we echo the strains of religious philosophy, based as much on Plato as on revelation in scripture: 'But the souls of the righteous are in the hands of God, and no torment shall touch them'. (Wisd. 3). The text assures us that in the eyes of the foolish they seemed to have died, that their departure from life was considered ruin, that they seemed punished in the sight of men, but that they are in peace, tried by God as men try gold in the furnace. They are accepted as a whole burnt offering. There is therefore a consolation for the diabolical holocaust: it is the most profound reversal, unimaginable in its consequences. It is the fulfilment of

Ezekiel's vision of the spirit-filled resurrection of scattered bones.

Atonement in the Spirit justifies the righteous and satisfies our moral demands. It removes from our painful existence the bewilderment of random terrors. As Christ suffered the pain and loss inflicted by the violation of justice, so even within the prescience of God the anonymous crowd of sufferers do not fall outside the orbit of providence. They are in peace. They are not alienated, lonely, abandoned souls but through the Spirit are brought into a unity, which is known in the gospels as the kingdom of God. The danger of subjectivity fades when the eternal life of the resurrected is reflected by each within the sacrificial energy of God himself. Thus Christian doctrine and human experience are crowned by a transcendent coherence, for all the aspects of institutional religion, of repentance and absolution, are lifted to an ultimate consummation. The life after death fulfils the vague presentiments of election and predestination: 'To them that love God all things work together for good, even to them that are called according to his purpose', (Rom. 8:28 ff.). Election is followed by justification and glorification.

Atonement in the Holy Spirit brings to us more than the salvation of souls. It rescues from perdition all the personal and supra-personal achievements and graces which would otherwise be lost in the transitoriness of time. Just as men are carried away in the floods of space and time, and as centuries bury with forgetfulness the humblest and the greatest, so also the spiritual towers and splendid tokens of genius vanish under layers of dust. The whole world threatens to become a cemetery, where there are interred heroic deeds and marvels of all kinds.

The two extreme wings of atonement theology meet in our conviction that 'nothing is lost'. On the one hand, recapitulation implies that the mills of God grind to dust only the perishable and that, as St Paul claimed, the genuine and real cannot vanish. Recapitulation consoles mankind for the transitoriness of people and achievements. It frees us from the constraints of history, for against the common view that time carries all its sons away into nothing it proclaims resurrection on a grand scale. The second pincer of atonement theology, namely satisfaction, also comes into play, for it widens its applicability. No longer are we concerned to stipulate conditionsfor God's satisfaction of justice, or our human hope for satisfaction. The two satisfactions turn out to be the same.

The abstract term 'union with God' is the umbrella for the total consummation in the future. It is a linguistic abstraction, almost devoid of meaning, until and unless it is seen in the context of atonement. The rehabilitation of living souls is for most people linked to faces known upon earth: children, parents, relations, friends, neighbours and possibly also enemies. We are certainly not dealing with skeletons in remembering and in being remembered. But this remembrance is only a starting point. It discloses a hierarchy of persons united to God and to each other, reflecting in one another the gifts and graces bestowed upon them. The union with God is neither abstract nor materialistically concrete: it transcends both and can only be articulated and perceived in iconography, poetry and musical polyphony.

Seen in this true light the sacrifice of Atonement no longer looks unbearable and ends our suspicion that humanity has been tricked in some sinister way. Yet only few men of genius and inspiration have been able to anticipate what 'we shall be' and that through the Incarnation of the Word we shall become like him who became like us. It requires a sinless view to enter into these depths of understanding which for most people can only come after this life on earth.

Yet I have seen this future on the uncelebrated faces of the humble and the suffering. The *Ecce homo* seems transfigured by the inwardness of their goodness. They anticipate the union with God because he dwells with and in them. Their inwardness opens their eyes to the glory of God. What they have seen, heard and handled is transformed into spiritual entity. They desire nothing for themselves. They enter into the strange reciprocity of love, where loving and being loved shares in the mystery of the Godhead.

Mystical theology describes this union with borrowed metaphors. The most impressive of all is the rose. The individual petals belong to, and radiate from, the stem of the bloom. But this metaphor, like all symbols, conceals more than it discloses, for it cannot and will not reveal the inner life, the invisible energy which unites each to all. For Dante, the circles of heaven, named after sun, moon and the planets, reach up to the Empyrean and the very heart of the universe.

The old slogans and concepts may now be safely abandoned. They have served their purpose up to a point. Justification by faith, for example, answers to the ordeals of conscience, but these ordeals are of the past, though remembered. The trials are over, the sinners are acquitted because they have accepted the sentence of mercy. The final state of atonement is union in which is also communion. Formerly unreconciled persons retain a past of contraries, but these are now contained in an immense variety. What seemed for ever polarised and heading for conflict becomes the reverse *sub specie aeternitatis*. The diversity derives from the gifts of the spirit and is as glorious as the stars in their courses or as the particles of the atom. One gives illumination to the other from the energy of the central source of light.

The structure in this unified multiformity is the reverse of power as abused on earth. Nothing is further from its essence than domination and envy. There is a hierarchical order, an ascending scale which may be compared to a ladder. But this ladder of perfection unites the perfected souls in an upward direction. Dante differentiated the ten heavens to stress the harmony of glorification, where the 'lowest' reflects the 'highest' without any awareness of privilege or the lack of it. Such a hierarchical structure, once it is perceived to be integral to the universe, causes wonderment. If we imagine the admission of the humblest on earth, such as the little laundress whom the Nazis executed for her compassion, to the splendour of renowned saints, of angels, archangels, cherubim and seraphim, and of the Virgin herself, words fail us. The common bond is grateful courtesy in this heavenly intercourse.

When atonement passes over into union we enter into that realm which St Paul knew to exceed everything known and experienced. Certainly we no longer care for the irritations and trivialities of daily life, and even the vindication of right against wrong no longer excites our main interest. Rather, as St John interpreted the glorification of Christ, the union itself is the fulfilment. The Father is glorified in the Son, and the Son is glorified in bringing mankind to the Father himself. But such a union is the very opposite of a totalitarian and faceless oneness. No ant-heap on earth can act as a simile of the spirit-filled diversity in unity. Indeed, one of the most intractable philosophical and religious problems, namely of the one and the many, can at last be understood as the very basis of reality. The endless numbers of beings, which Leibniz called monads, reflect one another in the infinite radiance of uncreated energy. Since the division of beings into 'high' and 'low' is done away, the monads retain their own characteristics without superiority or inferiority. All are in that sense one without surrendering their uniqueness: the personal and individual are eternalised in a new and growing existence. They retain a memory of what has been and what they have been, but they are now free from the constraints which were historical and tied to earthly events. Just as Jesus is seen to have 'ascended' beyond such a world of constraints, so the redeemed are bought out of the slavery into the freedom of the sons of God. This freedom naturally also includes the freedom from self-regard which has isolated individuals on earth in a kind of autistic self-separation.

Nevertheless this freedom from self must not be misunderstood as a kind of Nirvana or an absence of all desires. On the contrary, the freed multitude of souls are propelled by a purified desire to see God and to see one another. The meeting of former enemies need not be excluded; rather the fruit of forgiveness matures in such meetings which lie beyond the human imagination. Even within the family circle alienated husbands and wives, parents and children, brothers and sisters, must arrive at such a fulfilment of what 'they have always desired', as one prayer over the dead on earth has formulated the request. Clearly only the forgiven can forgive, and unless they forgive they are not forgiven.

This freedom to do and to receive clarifies another aspect of our existence and its consummation. On earth we are bundles of activity. After infancy and its sleep we grow not only in strength but in physical and mental quickness. This natural animation varies between individuals as well as races. It relates to the natural needs of propagation and the maintenance of life, property and industry, for the activity is always linked to real or imaginary wants and purposes.

But before long we discover that we cannot do as we would. External conditions of all kinds frustrate our natural desires. When we struggle with them we cannot control them. It seems that this frustration was accepted as natural in many societies and still is. In our peculiar western civilisation, however, frustration has led to aggressive and successful activism. Ever since adventurers set out for lands beyond the seas, the Faustian urge has battled against climatic, social, cultural and religious limits.

The technological advance would have been impossible apart from the freedom to experiment. It has also produced unforeseen consequences. Instead of uniting societies it has divided them. Instead of creating community it has alienated families and members of families. These well-known facts call out for atonement. We have lost the freedom to change ourselves and therefore are ourselves out of control.

In this unexpected way our freedom has produced its opposite. Our activism enforces a passive way of life. This enforced passivity is not unnatural, for both infancy and old age are cradled in sleep. Sleep itself is even for the most active adult a necessity and often a delight. Just as energy is positive and negative in electricity, the principle of activity-passivity operates in genuine freedom. Spiritual freedom accentuates the interplay of activity and passivity. On the simplest level prayer demonstrates the phenomenon; when man prays, even as a child, he or she resolves to do so. Physical postures go hand in hand with the formation of words and mental processes. At the same time the praying individual and society receive blessings in silence. The atoning union gives eternal validity to this interpenetration of active longing and passive receiving. For a Christian the communion is the archetype of this blending in which persons seek their incorporation in the universal and true home, the *Una Sancta* of God.

This infinite extension of the atonement embraces not only those unknown multitudes of human beings of all races and tongues which the Church celebrates on All Saints' Day and All Souls' Day, which surround the throne in circles of light and conscious delight. The whole universe is moved by the Atonement in vast energies released for spiritual perfection. In this movement the whole creation will be remade in fulfilment of the prophetic and apocalyptic vision. The whole process of aggression, catching, killing, eating and being eaten, with all the variations observed in insect and reptilian life and among mammals and birds, will be changed, and the war will cease. This utopian expectation, totally unrealistic on the earth we know, belongs to the reign of the spirit. Blake, among others, in verse and in engravings portrays the impossible made possible. This unrealistic and miraculous picture is necessary to place the consequences of atonement in the metaphysical realm. The old creation as given to us on earth simply cannot progress towards spiritual perfection and all our attempts at improvements, laws and inventions may be considered a holding operation. But the Christian claims of atonement break with props and barriers, for they speak of the new creation. The strains and stresses and extravagances, the boredoms and frustrations, the cycles of aggression and submission, on whatever levels, no longer divide because the same energies are controlled by that love which does not seek its own self-gratification.

At first this spiritual redirection seems to imply loss. Instead of the feverish activity familiar to us we are confronted by silence. There is no noise, no movement of barking and snapping dogs, of stalking cats, of whirring flies, or pushing and screaming humans. There is no action, no excitement. The union with God by the spirit separates us from the market-place and the factory and the word-processor. There is no programme and no competing voices or visuals penetrate the air. The *via negativa*, negative theology, hitherto only a phrase in a rare vocabulary, has become the road on which there is no need to travel. Such movements as exist are comparable to those in the stellar systems, in atoms and galaxies. The cosmic immensity does not thrive upon sensation or stimulus. The new creation breaks with the nervous fractions and spasms of the past.

No one has climbed to these stars of new existence more brilliantly than Dante, and no one has pictured this ascent more amazingly than Botticelli in his illustrations to the *Divine Comedy*. In Hell everything is noise, stench, thrusting, devouring, horror and suffering. The canvases are crowded beyond belief with naked ugliness and demonic snakes. This world is upside down and chaotic. Purgatory is the sphere of fire where sins are done away. The purged and penitent escape from the reign of pain in an orderly but still turbulent effort, following where led by grace, waiting and praying, wishing and learning. Here energies are being tamed, redirected and prepared. Memory, good and bad, is cleansed for radiance and new-heard melody.

Atonement in Heaven looks very different from what has gone before. The unspeakable wonder of love discloses a world so strange that Dante looks bewildered in the Circle of the Moon. We have every reason to rejoice in the unexpected, an element so often missing from theologies of justification and reconciliation. We are approaching the essence of reality, and the very heart of love. As the Holy Spirit leads the elect on this ascent Beatrice guides her friend. The emptiness of space is impressive; there is no more time. The blessed spirits express that what they desire they have, for 'in his will is our peace'. Each soul is satisfied completely, its capacity fulfilled, and since there is no unquenched thirst the emptiness around the spirits is really fullness. From now on the truth is to be seen, to be adored in contemplation: 'Here is what will give increase to our love', confess the spirits as splendours and

glories move towards them. Here at last honour and true
virtue have their own reward in seeing things as they are.
The Emperor Justinian explains to Dante the sweet
harmony of true justice. The just are as flames in the field
which are arranged in concentric circles, and it is here that
Beatrice dwells upon atonement, which comes from God's
justice and mercy shown in the Incarnation and the Passion
of his Son: 'God, in giving himself that man might be able
to raise himself, gave even more than if he had forgiven
him in mercy'. Ever pointing upwards, Beatrice leads
Dante into the Heaven of Venus, still surrounded in
emptiness by the fullness of fiery love. Nobility and
gentleness, not harshness or roughness, authorise royal
government, for thus divine providence orders the existence of individuals of whatever talents, the one with the
many.

This contentment of the many in the one is the gift of
the Holy Spirit. Pleasure and outward glow mirror the
inward disposition of each soul. Not fame but ardent
charity unites each to each and all to God. It is in the
Circle of the Sun that the imagery draws upon musical
harmony, for the radiance of the great spirits unites in
singing. As the naked eye cannot see into the heart of the
sun directly, so the truth of the eternal light is glimpsed
indirectly. Our experience of art is indeed an intimation
of that eternal light whose rays touch us in our finite state
but which, after God's reconciliation with us, become part
of us in infinity. Ezekiel's imagery of the wheel of fire
serves to portray the fiery unity composed of individual
radiances. How, since Dante's day, these individual
radiances have served the Holy Spirit, even to this present
moment! Modesty, not mine but theirs, forbids the naming
of names, but their intercessory power remains a proof of
atonement, theirs and ours.

Knowledge, scholarship and science penetrate the
darkness as much as humility, service and poverty. With
Dante, Dominic and Francis, compared to the cherubim
and seraphim, portray the heavenly rays of illumination.
Francis, the son of one Bernadone, on earth once a figure
of scorn and clad in rags, still reveals the regal dignity

despite his failure before the Sultan's power. Francis also then as now shows the stigmata, the wounds of Christ, in the glory. It is a strange double militancy for truth, intellectual and spiritual, which the Holy Spirit celebrates in such spirits made perfect.

The radiance of the sun lights up a plenitude of virtues which survive into the union with God. The dancing stars and the songs penetrate into the Godhead with a delicacy of understanding which theology often loses. True wisdom greets with delight the mystery of the three persons in one divine nature, and the divinity and humanity of Christ. Atonement itself would be meaningless unless it implied an entry into this mystery of the uncreated light. Botticelli again helps us poor denizens of earth to strip away all the camouflage of external events and trivial diversions to concentrate upon this one which is infinite. Atonement, let it be repeated, comes from God and leads to God, for each and all in communion.

More sparse becomes the detail as we approach the intersection of two rays of splendour, forming the cross. The red glow of Mars contains the light within itself, in which the blessed souls shine forth in eternal love. How far we are from justification, that deadly term of balances weighing guilt, when supreme love bestows wholly unearned splendour! But Dante still in thanksgiving insists on offering his soul as a burnt offering for this new bliss. Indeed, he makes us realise that sacrifice in the ultimate state is a permanent disposition of reverence. Like Dante we despair of finding metaphors to describe the state, for it is enough to worship and in worship to grow into closer and wider union.

All these metaphors and symbols are servants to express the inexpressible. They are at least more graphic and incisive than the empty word 'love'. Yet all treatments of the atonement of whatever schools agree that the saving initiative and its completion in union is caused by God's love, set forth in Jesus Christ and enacted by the Holy Spirit. But this agreement also leads to endless controversies, as between east and west, between tradition and modernity. The fundamental quest among theologians may be reduced to a fairly simple challenge, namely whether human love, as known on earth, reflects in any way this transcendent power. On the one hand the affirmations of human love lead to a sentimentalised pan-eroticism, whereas the negations separate the divine *Agape* totally from erotic relationships. The latter would exclude the very notion of happiness or pleasure as an ingredient of loving, such as experienced in the family and among friends. Infidelities, exploitations, ruptures and abuses of all kinds, found even among those who thought themselves in love and swore allegiance 'until death do us part', confirm the scepticism of books, such as Nygren's *Agape and Eros*. The trouble with the emerging concept of *agape* is its remoteness from sexuality and beauty. In the end the term *'agape'* stands for an abstraction without warmth.

In order to clarify the debate many works of the finest scholarship have been written on the subject of *agape*. It appears that even the Christians of the first century used it in a variety of ways. *Agape* as celebrated in 1 Corinthians may have converted the Corinthians to a level of understanding not previously approximated. On the other hand, when we look at 2 Corinthians, we may come to the conclusion that letters and advice often miss their mark. After all, *agape* is not a theoretical concept and is not meant to be one. Nor is it the kind of possession which can be handed on from generation to generation. As Christians succeeded in their missions and enlarged their institutions they often lost sight of *agape* as a token of eternal unity.

Much is made of the touching dialogue at the end of John's gospel when Jesus asks Peter 'Do you love me more than these?'. The verb in the question is *'agapan'* and Peter uses *'philein'* in response. Many sermons have been preached on this distinction, namely between *agape* and friendship. C.S. Lewis in his *The Four Loves*[1] has taken systematisation even further. Accordingly it may be held that even after the Atonement Christians react to reconciliation in varying degrees of love. But this approach is unsatisfactory, for it ignores the transcendental nature of *agape*. The 'highest gift' (1 Cor. 13:2) is 'of God to us and in us' (Rom. 5:5). This immanence of love derives from and reflects the love which unites the Son with the Father from the beginning of creation (John 17:26 and 1 John throughout). It is the gift of the Holy Spirit.

Atonement does not favour or imply sameness. Its centre is God's *Agape*, transcendental in every sense. Atonement derives from *agape* and far from reducing all to an equality of dullness it raises the spiritual monads to distinct entities. These are the 'faces' which Christian art celebrates in icons, frescoes, stained glass and sculptures. No martyr or saint is identical with another, though they resemble one another in their dedication to the truth. They radiate that light which 'darts across one arm of the cross, and down to its foot, like a spark behind alabaster'[2]. The happiness of the union by the Spirit always recalls that dedication, the sacrifice and the tears. The serene joy of these 'faces' may not exclude a knowledge of the demonic which they have overcome. We cannot lightly dismiss the certainty with which St Thomas Aquinas celebrates the victory of truth over the perverters of truth. To that extent the grim past reminds the souls that they were redeemed with a price. Even at the end of time the words from the Wisdom of Solomon, 'Love justice, you who judge the earth!', still have a ring of majestic authority: '*Diligite Iustitiam Qui Iudicatis Terram*' pertains to Dante's Heaven of Jupiter (Par. XV111. 91 ff.).

Atonement seen from above, transcendentally, is both formal and dynamic. The pictorial forms are associated with our redemption; they occur already in the Bible. Animals, birds and reptiles have come to symbolise aspects of the divine action. The Apocalypse connects the supremacy of the spirit with thrones, lightnings and thunders, lamps of fire and the four living creatures: lion, calf, man and eagle. The classical prophetic imagery, as in Isaiah 6 and Ezekiel 1, serves to illustrate atonement. The eagle, its great wings outspread, circles majestically with its message that God's justice surpasses the power of mortal reasoning. This justice is all-embracing and all-searing in loving retribution. The form of man with eye, ear, nose, breast, belly, thigh and feet is celebrated in the Song of Solomon. It stresses the beauty of the encounter in atonement, when eye meets eye and hand grasps hand.

The atoning and uniting love is not known in and by the world except in an oblique way. Neither the romantic passion in *Romeo and Juliet* nor the black parody of passion in *Troilus and Cressida* nor the suicidal despair in *Anna Karenina* point to anything except tragedy and death. All these fictional enlargements of human passion culminate in the very opposite of atonement. Yet Christian appraisal of marriage, monogamous and life-long, reaches out to the mystical love of Christ for his Church. Such a claim goes beyond human experience on earth. Vladimir Lossky summarises the orthodox way of union in terms of deification by *agape*. The Holy Spirit unites the free will of perfected souls with the divine will, for the soul which has renounced false desires is now free to be in love with the spirit of God. The heart is converted, not at the expense of the intelligence (*nous*) but rather by the raising of the contemplative faculty: 'Without the spirit, the heart remains blind'. In the uniting of action (*praxis*) and contemplation (*theoria*)man sheds empty fantasies and sterile knowledge and gains true discernment (*diakrisis*). But this mystical ascent relies upon the 'change of mind', the *metanoia*, and readiness to be re-made. *Metanoia* prepares the soul for union by prayer in the 'spiritual silence' which is sometimes identified with 'ecstasy'. The 'divine energy' inflames the soul and unites it to God in holy love. Thus the uncreated and 'very life of the divine nature' unites us to God. We become partakers of the divine nature, not in imitation of Christ but in a life in Christ[3].

Western mysticism is Jesus-centred. 'The whole contemplative life is required to issue in the unmitigated altruism of unwearying intercession, and the love that is like a smile'. St Bernard of Clairvaux insists that 'the bridal chamber must be strewn with the flowers of good works before the Bridegroom will visit it'. Both the religious in monasteries and the men and women in the world must be morally trained to find rest with the bride-

groom of the soul, Jesus known in his humanity. 'My
beloved is a bundle of myrrh, he shall lie between my
breasts', preaches the saint from the Song of Solomon and
keeps the text as an amulet. The name of Jesus is the
saving medicine and the falling in love enables the soul to
resist evil and to be united with God. The metaphors of
the Song of Solomon retain their erotic resonance as they
are freed from lust and directed towards the true goal of
atonement.

St Bernard stands at the centre of a traditional spirituality
when he preaches on the Song of Solomon; at the start, on
'Let him kiss me with the kiss of his mouth', he comments:
'Who speaks? The bride. Who is she? The soul thirsting
for God . . . Words cannot be found so sweet as to express
the sweet affections of the Word and the soul for each
other, except bride and Bridegroom'. There is beauty
throughout, the image of eternity. External appearances
may deceive the eye, but the inward reality unites 'My
beloved to me and I to him'. The flame of mutual love
enlightens the soul to see God. St Paul gave final expression
to the supremacy of divine love which remains when
everything else has passed away (1 Cor. 13).

God chooses the redeemed souls for ecstasy. Like gems
they sparkle in the divine light which they reflect. Their
eyes behold the radiance at the centre of all things. They
soar upwards in the traffic of the celestial ladder, with
their gentle smiles meeting the warm benevolence of the
fire. This fire does not burn and destroy but constantly
feeds the love from which all things spring. Humans
swoon at so much, such abundant energy, for it cannot be
measured. It blinds the unprepared and frightens the
unworthy. None can hide from the power of the pure,
rational, loving being around which the redeemed company circle in adoration and with great joy. Here at last is
the substance of what we hope to see and the argument
for what we have not seen. The indissoluble unity of faith,
hope and love dazzles the soul with the unapproachable
holiness of God himself and so the soul returns to its
maker in paradise. We become sparks within this brilliant
incandescence to complete the cosmic order.

It remains incomplete without music. At the end the heavenly choirs are heard in hymns of adoration[4]. As music points to, adorns and is part of reality we may well conclude that elements of time and dynamics are built into the universe to which we become reconciled by God. Music is unthinkable without divisions and distinctions, modes and modulations. Even the most straightforward incantation, prayers intoned on one note, leads into vast complexities which are related to vibrations. On earth we apply mathematical principles to measure musical proportions. Even the shepherd's flute on a hillside shares in a scientific wonder integral to reconciliation and atonement.

Most Christians and many non-Christians are indeed 'converted' by the voice of music. Poets acclaim music as the handmaid of God, and it is not difficult to see why. For some, hymns of praise are a transport beyond themselves and hymns which intone penitence arouse contrition. The community of faith enjoys its identity in singing and this, in its turn, must evoke all levels of reconciliation. But the atoning effect of music does not stop within church or chapel walls. Words do not have to be understood in order to do the strange work. The music itself, divorced from all dogmatic statements, elevates the soul.

Once again we are confronted by inequalities and degrees of grace. The one unspeakable glory is communicated in more variety than the prisms of light. Even one set piece of music is never the same for two performances; it depends on the artistic performance and the physical and spiritual circumstances of the audience. But far greater than these uncertainties and ambiguities is the problem of the moral content of music. Right at the start, from our observations and anthropology, we note that music underpins doubtful enterprises. Human aggression prospers when the same rhythm beats away in ever-accelerating ferocity. Wars and terror are 'inspired' by singing and the endless repetition of militant bars. None of our contemporary tyrannies are thinkable apart from their own hymns, the musical adulation of state and tyrant. The Nazis' *Horst-Wessel-Lied* and their *'Wir fahren gegen Engeland'* induced states of paroxysm. Pandemonium is found at pop concerts in these latter days. The Sex Pistols shoot out ecstatic invitations to a dance of hell. Music has been and still is the greatest enemy to atonement when it is in the power of devils.

One need not go to extremes to find music an ally to spiritual destruction. The writers and makers of the Christian and humanistic tradition could never have had a notion of how the sweet companion of our souls could be brought low to meaninglessness. The mechanisation of sound must be the major cause, but its use goes back to human determination to opt for evil rather than good. Thus shops and even places of business throb with a meaningless rhythm and hotel lifts go up and down to meaningless musak, tapes and more tapes unwinding to bring 'background' to the empty mind and the void of the soul. Whether loud or soft, fast or slow, produced live or reproduced, this sort of music devalues the greatest potential of the divine spirit in us.

Atonement in music, however, also abounds and is heard and appreciated by many. The great scenes of opera provide the most accessible material, for here the texts demand appropriate settings in duets or other ensembles. It is impossible to give here a catalogue of such invasions of the human scene of strife by the most moving and reconciling spirit. Mozart in *Figaro* ends this *opera buffa* on a high note of repentance and pardon, as Count and Countess Almaviva come together after complicated plots and counterplots. Mozart transcends the immediacy of the plot and the stage becomes that of all humanity with its deceits and dividing lusts and ambitions. 'Angel, forgive me' is a sincere cry from the heart, even if we may doubt that it can be the last one. But it is the music which lifts us from the ordinariness to the extraordinary, from the sins of the flesh to the spirit.

Verdi is the composer who approaches reconciliation outside religious conventions with unique passion. His constant preoccupation with Shakespeare's and Schiller's tragedies recreated the plays as operas with a difference. Whereas the great tragedies of the theatre cannot end in reconciliation, since all the heroes die and are thus out of this world, Verdi's libretti are so structured that reconciliation comes before death and with great pain. Whereas Othello cannot undo the killing of Desdemona, the wronged men and women, parents and sons and daughters, can come together before death. Even in *Don Carlos* reconciliation between the Prince and Posa and the Queen lights up the sombre finale with a mystical dawn of atonement. The libretti serve the music, and the astonishing blending of opposing voices, especially in *Simone Boccanegra*, moves the heart to an unknown dimension of tenderness. Here is forgiveness in a secular dress, complete and unalloyed.

The place of texts in vocal compositions is always ambiguous. Even what we consider to be poor, sentimental or downright bad lyrics may stir the heart and create a longing for reconciliation. It is one of the ironies of our musical culture that the best poems do not make the best songs. Schubert's best *lieder* are not the settings of Goethe but of Müller. As regards English church music, the hymns appointed for Passiontide are a medley of the best and of the worst. The popular 'When I survey the wondrous cross', for example, has a sugary taste, whereas the famous Bach chorales, though originally folk songs, furnish Good Friday services with a theology of the atonement.

The texts are certainly prior to the music. The psalms had already gained the central place in worship before the foundation of the Church. For centuries the Church used the psalms without embellishment. The Gregorian chant united singers and worshippers in the belief that God forgives sins and grants reconciliation to all who seek it. It can still be heard in the churches where Latin prevails in the liturgical offices. Once the language is 'modernised' the spell seems to be broken. This is certainly odd when one considers that the psalms were for centuries read and sung in Hebrew. Yet the Latinisation in the west has become inseparable from Gregorian chant.

With the arrival of polyphony the relationship between words and music changed, and the psalms were soon heard in the tongues of the people. Polyphony enhanced the power of the liturgical order and did not kill the transcendent character of the texts. The psalms in congregational singing opened heavenly dimensions to the warring factions on earth. From Benedictine Latin to American-English we follow a marked change, though the words are really the same. The celestial harmony is not yet exhausted by earthly approximations.

In this monumental treasure house of transcendent compositions, atonement naturally descends upon the listener most directly when the *Kyrie eleison*, the *Qui tollis* and the *Agnus dei* are sung. All these liturgical texts are essentially prayers. But the music objectifies the statements and imperatives so that we feel, quite rightly, that what is sung on earth shares in the choirs of heaven. Who but the most unmusical and insensitive can fail to be 'atoned' by being attuned to the great masses of Haydn? Only recently have we become familiar with this amazing polyphony in which the Catholic tradition has attained to its highest perfection. These masses are not congregational or meant to be sung by all and sundry; they have to be rehearsed carefully, not only by the choirs, but by the soloists and the orchestra. When the liturgy begins in church there is clearly not a feeling of a concert performance; the centrality of the altar with the atoning sacrifice together with the configurations of pillars and statues and stained glass windows opens to the faithful a direct presence of God himself in his trinitarian self-giving. A more perfect partaking of future bliss does not exist on earth.

The secularisation of this music in concert halls is a simple fact, just as the distribution of the music reaches all purchasers of recordings on discs, tapes and cassettes. The burden of participation becomes very complex. This challenge to personal concentration upon sacred music never existed in the pre-technological age. Examples showing that even transcendent music can be heard as 'background' music bring to one's mind the warning that pearls must not be cast before undiscerning swine. At a Baltimore dinner party Mozart's *Requiem* was 'put on' and meant as a favour to myself.

But atonement is so uncertain a substance that no one

knows in advance what are the pearls and who are the swine. The recipients of grace always insist that they are unworthy. The effect of transcendent music is very often received outside churches and within a secular setting. I heard Bach cantatas first in a concert hall, and my auditory illumination was both instantaneous and lasting. Bach's music is *sui generis* and directly communicates penitence, forgiveness, union with and in Christ, praise and consummation. The texts may be taken from the Catholic liturgy, or from Protestant pietism, or the music may be wordless. Bound neither by denominational narrowness nor by general sentimentality, Bach takes the musical pilgrim by the ear into a universe of sound even more complex than the ten heavens of classical theology.

Musicology, often vilified as an arid science, helps us to get some glimpse of this miracle which is given to Bach by the Holy Spirit. It is perhaps appreciated best at its least openly religious. The concertos (Brandenburg, those for one or several pianos or harpsicord, for oboe and violin, for solo violin and for solo cello, the Musical Offering, the Art of Fugue) proved that texts are not necessary to make heavenly music. Even merely looking at the score, if possible the autographs (mostly in Berlin), presents to the eye what is meant to be mediated to the ear. Perfect order, mathematical precision, harmonies and disharmonies, modulations, contrasts of all kinds, can be seen to build this monument to unspoken and unspeakable truth. It need not be analysed to enter the soul, though some sort of participation hastens the response. Here is the hidden God in self-disclosure ready to embrace the unworthy.

The technical intricacies of Bach's music may be compared to those of the atonement itself. A detailed examination of counterpoint alone would demand a thesis as long as that concerning the world-wide use and psychology of the scapegoat. But the outstanding feature of Bach's inspiration by God is his contribution to the ordering of the chaotic, the imposition of the ideal on the material, the beauty of the multidimensional in music. One Bach fugue may open the portals of salvation to the soul which responds with awe and alacrity. Bach seems to answer Kafka's quest in *The Trial*, when the door to justice, so the priestly narrator says, has always been open to the comer, of whom nothing is demanded except to go in and pass through. Bach's doors, however, do not shut but remain open on the way to God.

The open road to atonement and the extremely complex substance of atonement can only be stated musically, and Bach is the supreme master of this statement, because it is from above, from outside, spirit-in-matter. Hence we see two sides which seem in our experience paradoxes. On the one hand, Bach's music is abstract and entirely objective, appealing to no particular sentiment and promising no rewards. On the other hand, no one can hear Bach without responding personally to this entirely objective fact. Such objectivity and individuality come together to a certain extent in all good art, and in music above all; but Bach discloses the paradox not as another ingredient, but as the very substance of reality. It is the music of reconciliation, essentially, formally, existentially.

Later priests of music still combine this objectivity with existential response, spirit calling spirit from the deep. Darker shades and tragic accents reach our ears, but they still speak of eternity and a yearning for redemption. Mozart is rightly loved for his beyond time and space music. If it is to reconcile us to things in this world it must be by the disclosure of paradise. Menacing are his G minors and D minors in quartets, quintets, the kyries of the Mass in C minor and the haunting *Requiem*. This menace leads to wonder, amazement, petition, silence, before the soul can hope for consolation. There is none of Haydn's assurance and natural good nature, but Mozart also transcends doubt and terror on our behalf.

Doubt and terror become ever more audible in our time; they press for a response to the soul, storming or laying siege to the invisible God. We have to accept the longing as the token of the presence of the spirit of God, as in Beethoven's *Missa Solemnis* and the late quartets. Again the only hope is beyond hope. The music itself must be the substitute for hope and for despair, and at the end thanksgiving remains: *gratias tibi agimus*. Verdi unleashes his *Requiem*, which measures the chaos of our day which he anticipates. Enmeshed in the struggle for liberation he can still set forth on behalf of Manzoni the text of the *Dies Irae*, which promises requiem despite the turmoil of all around and within. We can only tremble at the thought that the prisoners of Theresienstadt gave a performance under the aegis of their captors and tormentors before and in sight of extermination. '*Rex tremendae maiestatis*' is uttered on behalf of the whole world.

The continuity of the atoning work is not in the hands of man. Human attempts at reconciliation seem fallible, often tragically ineffective, unpredictable, contingent. The atoning work of God is sovereign and providential, free from the contingencies of error. Past, present and future are comprehended in the prayer of realisation:

O God, who hast prepared for them that love thee such good things as pass man's understanding: Pour into our hearts such love toward thee, that we, loving thee above all things, may obtain thy promises, which exceed all that we can desire; through Jesus Christ our Lord.

Grant, we beseech thee, merciful Lord, to thy faithful people, pardon and peace.

The paradox of Atonement

I have written the above, and you may have read it, while guns blaze, bombs explode, the innocent are arrested, victims disappear, false reports circulate, children are violated, secrets betrayed. The list of human misdeeds and sufferings is endless. Not a single line of this book will lead to our reconciliation to the horrors around us. Our human history is no longer on a small scale, of little dots on the map, but embraces the continents, the seas and the spheres. Nowhere do we find evidence for consolation.

The despair is to be contrasted with the hope which shines through the darkness. There is virtue to be found among the true and the faithful, who repair the material and mental damage, mediate between warring factions, feed the hungry, visit the prisoners, intercede for the innocent. Some religious bodies and churches devote their energies to bringing peace and reconciliation on all levels of conflict. From racial confrontations to domestic strife they touch upon points of violence to disarm aggressors.

Neither the despair nor the hope relate directly to Christian atonement, which must be exclusive and transcendental. The Jesus of Nazareth cannot leave the Galilean past and the crucifixion in Jerusalem; the Christ ascends above time and space. The so-called theories of atonement are formulated around the work of Jesus Christ, the man in history and the risen one beyond. His moral example, his payment for debt, his exposure of demonic nothingness, his act of reparation and satisfaction and final recapitulation of mankind in the restored creation, baffle our contemporaries.

This is not surprising in an age which is post-Christian and outside the context of creation, redemption, and salvation. Non-Christian religions either shun the very notion of reconciliation (Islam) or prefer ways of abnegation (Buddhism), whereas the secular humanists react almost angrily to Christian claims. The media in the west spread a cynical and sardonic attitude, which in condoning strife and controversy with professional assiduity cannot be expected to respond to the appeal 'be reconciled' on any level whatsoever. Communist (Marxist-Leninist) theorists and propagandists denounce these appeals as 'mystical', i.e. unreal and counter-revolutionary. Churches have been infiltrated by priests and theologians who respond to the Marxist dismissal by refining a purely socialist stance as the equivalent of traditional atonement.

The most difficult and lasting gulf separates the Jews from the Christian claims. Though they have given to the Church the categories of *Kipper* and the *Pesach* and the whole sacrificial context of the *Aqedah* and the martyred servant, they shrink from extending these ideas and emblems to Jesus Christ and to Christian claims. Indeed, they reject them on the basis of historical experience, though some outstanding Jews (St Teresa of Avila, Mandelstamm, Edith Stein, Raissa Maritain, Levertoff, etc.) ignored the effects of the Inquisition, pogroms and humiliations in the name of the crucified and risen one. Since Auschwitz a new spirit rules, reconciliation is not impossible, but a truce obtains rather than a deep understanding on both sides.

We are trapped through and in our history. Wherever we look for an escape we find the exits barred, for prejudices and hatreds built up in time refuse to come out of time. Therefore bombs are considered more relevant than transcendent truth. But we are also trapped because the documents relating to atonement are themselves of the past and require an understanding of the past from generations which are now alienated from the past. There is a notable difference between the Hitler-Goebbels-Goering attitude to Christian claims – they knew them, rejected them and would annihilate them – and the modern Marxists, for they have a dialectic which includes the past and consider it irrelevant to the victorious class-struggle. Many contemporary Christians are Marxists and, like them, show themselves incapable of understanding the past. The language, the forms of presentation and the feeling are so remote from their thought forms that they cannot grasp the content. The historical framework ruins the perception within history even among well-wishers who have no reason to oppose reconciliation.

This is the heart of the problem. We have seen that not such a long time ago solutions were found. Even in the nineteenth century with its sweep of Darwinism, theologians such as Rashdall and Moberly could reinterpret the Atonement by accommodating the new modes of thought in traditional outlines. As we have seen, psychology and psychoanalysis could at least approach reconciliation in terms borrowed from antiquity and from the Bible.

We also use the same approach. We continue to be grounded in the world, which we think real and therefore historical, because people live in it. As individuals or as members of societies they fall into the pattern of reconciliation. They have eyes and ears and noses, they have faces and bodies, emotions and reasons. As such they reflect the kind of life and its needs which connects with strife, suffering, yearning and achieving. As long as people want to pay or be paid compensation, engage a solicitor to plead and a witness to propitiate angry antagonists, seek to be avenged for wrongs endured, to be justified in court, to be acquitted and rewarded, they stand within the framework of setting things right. As long as people go so far as to look for a reprieve, a merciful cover for misdeeds, a leaping-over hurdles which divide or threats which offend, actively or passively they are acting out some form of atonement, even though they may not be conscious of that. Even the scapegoat is still in our midst in our concern to identify guilty and innocent people. Thus the ancient, the mythological and the historical converge upon our living experience.

However, it is the anticipation of death, i.e. the vanishing from the historical world, which gives power to our quest. Death opens up the perspective of absolute nothingness, the fear of the unknown beyond nothingness, the possibility of meaning beyond meaninglessness. Dying is a process before death which ends the theorising, even if medicine as the new magic and doctors as the new priests have taken the awe out of the awful.

Death has always challenged religions and philosophical speculations. 'Welcome, death' has always been opposed by 'alas, death'. The longing for peace and atonement has always been lodged between these two emotions. But now the paradox has become far more extreme. On the one hand, the new magic of life-preserving medicine has neutralised the subject, as if we were meant to live for ever, and Marxist materialism has simply nothing to say on the subject, thereby dismissing the problem. Bodies decompose and the molecules do their job mechanistically. On the other hand, the outrages, atrocities and sufferings on a huge scale, have given a new dimension to death. The welcome to the termination of the ordeal, from arrest to torture to humiliation to starvation, also demands a reconciliation with the whole human condition, the injustice which so blatantly has robbed mankind of all hope.

This moral yearning for vindication vibrates through all the pages and recorded voices of our time. Until recently death itself could be accepted as natural, indeed with a lyrical tone of gratitude, when sickness and old age followed infancy and youth. But now both sated with, and shocked by, unnatural death, our moral indignation fuels the spiritual hunger which underlies the quest for reconciliation, not with man but with God. Whereas a Job was cast into the role of accuser and rose above his leprous state by seeking and finding redemption, the contemporary

Jobian masses can engage in no such dialogue, since the absent God is not known, and hence confusion reigns, leading to despair.

The theories of the atonement provide a way out of this confusion. They focus on the death of Jesus as a necessary and historical event on the one hand, and as a transcendent meta-historical reality on the other. They enable us to see this death as human martyrdom. When we reflect on the death of Jesus we look at the face of the dying man. We are subjective observers and continue to be subjective in endeavouring to enter into his experience. Though we cannot really know how Jesus felt during the hours on the cross we identify them with the ordeals which thousands have endured throughout history. The Via Appia outside Rome was a place where many victims were executed in this cruel manner. But our identifications extend to the present time and also to the past. We cite the examples of Socrates and of Bonhoeffer. We make death more subjective and perhaps more acceptable by associating the annihilation with a person in the drama of history. Our tradition in the west is rich in directing our imagination. We look at pictures, frescoes and statues which commemorate men and women who died in a good cause. Michelangelo's Pieta is one of many memorials which move us not only with pity but also with hope. All deaths in Shakespearean tragedies are notable because they touch our innermost being.

This subjectivity, implicit in the observer's vision and understanding, pairs with the objectivity of death itself. This paradox is not unknown in science, where it is generally claimed that the observer or experimenter cannot be excluded but is part of the observed experiment. The theories of the atonement tend to stress the objective at the expense of the subjective. Nevertheless, following the New Testament they attach to the death of Jesus a uniqueness which can never be lost. The I-Thou relationship remains prominent in all liturgical prayers, for they are directed to God 'through Jesus Christ'. When we seek after reconciliation we are more impressed by this personal address than by the objective language of reparation and satisfaction.

The tension subjectivity-objectivity does not seem to have worried previous generations. When a creed begins: 'Credo in unum Deum' the whole problem seems to be solved, at least as a matter of language. In one short phrase you state your commitment, realising that it is also that of others before and after you, and happily proceed to the area of your belief: God. The latter need not be defined, but God is certainly 'objective' in the sense of being beyond experience, beyond time, space and human control. The clauses regarding atonement come in the same breath of confession. The relevant phrases are introduced by the relative 'qui' – 'Crucifixus etiam pro nobis sub Pontio Pilato passus, et sepultus est'. This sounds very existential and subjective, but it is not, for 'crucified, suffered, buried' is now articulated as a fact. It is both a fact in history, under Pontius Pilate, and also it is confessed as an objective truth beyond history.

Modernistic interpretations of the Atonement have instinctively followed a subjective line. But this is now seen to fail. Unless Jesus is raised by God and thus translated as the pre-existent word into the eternal kingdom, his death cannot be more than a fleeting impression. Thus a painter, like Kokoschka, may paint Jesus on the cross with one hand free to bless the starving children after 1945. But this is typically subjective imagination, impressive, touching, but lacking in objective verity. When a symbol takes leave of historical moorings it may also fail as an indicator of objective truth.

Concentration camps may be said to have ended the subjective phase. The prisoners even to this day are stripped of their identity. Nothing is left to them. The moral example of Jesus remains hidden whereas the demonic nothingness presses upon the damned who torture, and the condemned who suffer. At times a glimmer of light shines through the walls and the wires, for acts of kindness still occur and the stars sparkle in the immense skies above. The only hope is that 'out there' the truth will prevail, the right will be vindicated. This 'out there' is anti-historical, untouched by and victorious over all the smears and lies of degraded mankind. 'Credo' would be an empty phrase apart from the eternal power which entered the historical process to redeem and end it. The final recapitulation of mankind in the restored creation fulfils God's promise.

The final paradox consoles us. We have been divided in ourselves. We have encountered hostilities on all possible fronts. Debts and liabilities have mounted, resentments and hatred have darkened the whole world. Whole communities have been wiped out and the innocent have cried out against the murderers. The criminal powers have not repented and the rule of the lie has maintained itself by force and terror. This demonic empire is now seen to be empty, bent upon its own destruction. It is exposed to the truth. The silence of the redeemed creation stops the devilish noise. The creator creates a new world, the redeemer unites the redeemed with himself, and the spirit fills the elect with eternal life.

I officiate in a church in London dedicated to the first British martyr, a Roman soldier. The huge panel behind the altar depicts a scene in which victims of genocide expire behind bars, starved into submission. They join a throng of the lame, the halt, the beaten and the poor. Together they ascend with priests and sages, women of all ages and the hierarchies of heaven to the centre of being.

NOTES

SECTION I

Chapter 6
1   i.e. the ultimate removal of the chain being brought about
    by the fall. In this restoration through successive universes
    even the devil and the demons attain salvation.

SECTION III

Chapter 10
1   *Apology*, 30.

Chapter 11
1   The memorial commemorates the names of some 2500
    victims guillotined or hanged there. The exhibition is in the
    Stauffenbergstr. 14. The printed pamphlet in English gives
    details.

Chapter 14
1   *De Trin.* I, iii, 5.

Chapter 16
1   C. S. Lewis, *The Four Loves*, Geofrey Bles, London, 1960. Cf.
    also M. C. D'Arcy, *The Mind and Heart of Love. A study in Eros
    and Agape*, Faber & Faber, London, 1945.
2   K. Clark, *The drawings by Sandro Botticelli for Dante's Divine
    Comedy*, Thames & Hudson, London 1976, p. 184, Pl. XV.
3   Cf. V. Lossky, *The Mystical Theology of the Eastern Church*,
    1957, James Clarke & Co, Cambridge.
4   E.g. Dante in the *Divine Comedy*, Purg. ii. 112–4; Par, xxiii,
    97ff.

BIBLIOGRAPHY

Gustav Aulen, *Christus Victor*, London, SPCK, 1931

Karl Barth, *Church Dogmatics IV, Part 1, The Doctrine of Reconciliation*, Edinburgh, T & T Clark, 1956

James Denney, *The Christian Doctrine of Reconciliation.* London, Hodder & Stoughton, 1917

F. W. Dillistone, *The Christian Understanding of Atonement*, London, Nisbet, 1968

Martin Hengel, *The Atonement*, London, SCM, 1981

Henry McKeating, *Living with Guilt*, London, SCM, 1986

Frances Young, *Sacrifice and the Death of Christ*, London, SPCK, 1975

Holocaust and Genocide Studies, 1986ff., Oxford

Index